# RELATIVITY

### IN

# MAN AND SOCIETY

# RELATIVITY
## IN
# MAN AND SOCIETY

BY

ARTHUR F. BENTLEY

*New Introduction by*

Sidney Ratner, *Rutgers University*

1968
**OCTAGON BOOKS, INC.**
*New York*

*Reprinted 1968*
*by special arrangement with Julius Altman*

**OCTAGON BOOKS, INC.**
175 Fifth Avenue
New York, N. Y. 10010

Library of Congress Catalog Card Number: 68-21839

*Printed in U.S.A. by*
NOBLE OFFSET PRINTERS, INC.
NEW YORK 3, N. Y.

# INTRODUCTION TO THE OCTAGON EDITION
by
Sidney Ratner*

The increasingly wide-spread interest in Bentley's writings, once known only to a small critical elite, has resulted in this new edition of *Relativity in Man and Society*. Syracuse University during the past academic year (1966–67) organized a Bentley Seminar to evaluate the Great Society program of President Johnson in all its phases, domestic and foreign. A volume embodying the lectures by eminent scholars from all parts of the United States will be published this year, with an essay on, and a tribute to, Bentley.[1]

Arthur F. Bentley was born in Freeport, Illinois, Oc-

---

*Professor of History, Rutgers University; Editor, *Inquiry Into Inquiries* by Arthur F. Bentley (Boston: Beacon Press, 1954) and co-editor, *John Dewey and Arthur F. Bentley, A Philosophical Correspondence 1932–1951* (New Brunswick: Rutgers University Press, 1964).

[1] Bertram Gross, ed., *A Great Society?* (New York: Basic Books, 1968).

iii

tober 16, 1870, the son of Charles Frederick and Angeline Alice (Fisher) Bentley. His father, a small-town banker, was a man of unusual ability and candor. Arthur Bentley obtained his early education in the public schools of Freeport, Illinois, and Grand Island, Nebraska. After studying for over a year at York College, Nebraska, and the University of Denver, he worked for three years in his father's bank. At twenty he entered Johns Hopkins University, with economics as his major interest. After two years he was graduated in 1892 with high honors and an A.B. degree. He also wrote a scholarly monograph, "The Condition of the Western Farmer as Illustrated by the Economic History of a Nebraska Township," which was published in 1893 in the *Johns Hopkins Studies in Historical and Political Science.*

From 1892 to 1895 he did graduate work in economics and sociology, two years at Johns Hopkins and a year in Germany, mainly at the University of Berlin. In 1895 he received the Ph.D. degree from Johns Hopkins, with a thesis, "The Units of Investigation in the Social Sciences." This thesis focused on the human mind as central to all study of social phenomena and embodied a mentalistic approach that he in a few years rejected strenuously.

After one year's experience as a lecturer in sociology

at the University of Chicago in 1895–96, Bentley gave up an academic career and spent the next fifteen years in the newspaper world, first as a reporter, then as an editorial writer, on the Chicago *Times-Herald* and the *Record-Herald*. There he witnessed at first hand the stormy, diverse political activities that embodied conflicting group interests. As a consequence of this exposure to the brutal facts of public life, Bentley wrote his first great work, published in 1908, *The Process of Government*.[2]

Though unappreciated by the general public for some time, this book came to be acclaimed as one of the great classics in political science. Bentley's profound analysis of "group interests" behind the legislative, administrative, and judicial activities of governments became a basis for the massive research work done on pressure groups by Charles Beard, Arthur Holcombe, Peter Odegard, and Pendleton Herring, among others. But Bentley defined "group interests" in the light of the diverse activities and objectives of human beings. His approach was more flexible and pluralistic than that of the static "interest groups" of established political scientists as late as the 1930's and 1940's.

In 1910 Bentley left Chicago and the world of jour-

------

[2] The latest edition was edited by Peter H. Odegard (Cambridge, Mass.: The Belknap Press of Harvard University Press, 1967).

nalism to establish himself outside the town of Paoli, Indiana. There he built up his health by managing for a time an apple orchard and then carried on a very active life of research and writing for over forty years. Nevertheless, he retained a keen interest in political and world affairs, from Wilson's New Freedom to F.D.R.'s New Deal and Truman's Fair Deal. In 1920 Bentley completed but did not publish a book on the dominance of Big Business in the economic and political spheres of American life, *Makers, Users, and Masters.* In 1924 he engaged in practical politics and helped carry on in Indiana a campaign for the election of Robert La Follette as President.

During the early 1920's Bentley became impressed by the implications for the social sciences of Einstein's revolutionary work on the theory of relativity. In 1926 *Relativity in Man and Society* was published. Sociologists, Bentley contended, should emulate the physicists in discarding Newton's absolute space and time and adopt instead Einstein's scientifically fruitful way of viewing space and time as dimensions or integral phases of the events experienced and studied by human beings. Bentley did not go into the complexities of Einstein's work, as physicists like P. W. Bridgman or specialists in the philosophy of science like Adolf Grunbaum were later to do.[3] But Bentley was profoundly correct in seeing the need for sociologists to introduce their own observational position in space–time and society as a necessary element in all their reports on social events.

A great need existed in the 1920's for removing confusions created by such ambiguities as the mind–body terminology in psychology or the individual–society formulation in sociology. Bentley did this by presenting a new frame of reference for sociological inquiry. To replace the established dichotomy between the individual and society he offered the new term "man–society" as designating a field for investigation, with stress on the relation of each person to specific groups. Each social fact or situation should be understood as a "cross-section of activity" occurring in a group of human beings. This cross-sectional approach was an outgrowth of the group-activity analysis he had set forth in *The Process of Government.* (In the 1940's he used the term "transaction" as a replacement for both these earlier phrases.)

In recent years social scientists have debated the mer-

---

[3] Cf. P. W. Bridgman, *The Logic of Modern Physics* (New York: Macmillan, 1927); Adolf Grünbaum, *Philosophical Problems of Space and Time* (New York: Knopf, 1963); and Paul A. Schilpp, ed., *Albert Einstein: Philosopher-Scientist,* 2 vols., Harper Torchbook (New York: Harper, 1959).

its of methodological individualism against those of methodological collectivism or holism. In brief, the issue is whether large-scale social events and conditions should be treated as simple "aggregates or configurations of the actions, attitudes, relations, and circumstance of the individuals who participated in, enjoyed, or suffered them." Methodological individualists like Karl Popper and J. W. N. Watkins say we should. Methodological holists like Ernest Gellner and Maurice Mandelbaum maintain that social phenomena may be studied at their own independent, macroscopic level of analysis. Social "wholes" (systems or subsystems) are the "true" historical individuals.[4]

The merit of Bentley's position in this work is that he avoids the limitations of both schools. He rejects the idea that social groups or classes are more or less fixed entities as well as the thesis that persons exist as social atoms, independently of groups. To him each human being has diverse interests that he seeks to satisfy by taking joint action with others. He is a member of as many groups as he has interests. Bentley saw the advantage of stressing group action and behavior, but he never neglected the special drives or qualities of the persons who formed, created, or led different groups.

---

[4] Cf. W. H. Dray, "Holism and Individualism," *Encyclopedia of Philosophy,* Paul Edwards, ed., 8 vols. (New York: *Macmillan Free Press,* 1967), 4:53–58.

# Introduction

Another enduring contribution of *Relativity in Man and Society* is Bentley's explication of "social relativism." Every statement people make about social facts and values, e.g., the alleged inferiority of non-Aryans to Aryans, needs to be given with reference to the conditions of its origin and use, e.g., the desire of the Nazi party members to dominate first Germany and then Europe. If the special ethnic, economic, and cultural position of each commentator on social questions is given, then the bias of each person and group can be corrected. Moreover, the conflicting views on different social issues can be explained, and the reasons therefore can be communicated from one group to another. Thereby the type of objectivity and understanding of different perspectives held by different observers in physics can be approximated by sophisticated social scientists, despite their class, national, and racial differences.

Some critics of Bentley have accused him of being too socially detached from the social conflicts of his time. Actually he was deeply concerned about these conflicts. But he consciously sought to be scientifically "neutral" in expounding the diversity of group interests on economic, social, or political problems. As a good cultural pluralist he realized that different groups have their own values, and he criticized all classes, nations, and races that tried to force their rule and values on other groups.

Yet he felt the desirability of preventing future wars, even though the odds against achieving world peace were very great. He also wished for economic reforms that would limit the power of Big Business and improve the lot of the working and middle classes. In short, Bentley had his own values, but like Dewey he stressed the values of intelligent reform based on group persuasion, group pressure, and utilization of all the resources of representative government.

After 1926 Bentley devoted himself to working out in technical detail the basis for a methodology and philosophy of scientific inquiry. In 1932 he published a formidable treatise on the nature of meaning and postulates in science, particularly in mathematics, entitled *Linguistic Analysis of Mathematics.* Three years later he elaborated his views on the proper methods for studying human behavior in *Behavior, Knowledge, Fact.* These two volumes were appreciated by a small but choice group of readers. John Dewey found them of great value in clarifying his ideas on the autonomy of logic (or scientific method) and on the importance of the space–time component in each scientific statement of fact.

As a result of Dewey's interest in Bentley's later writings, they collaborated in writing *Knowing and the Known,* a milestone in the development of naturalism and pragmatism. Their volume centered on the need for a re-examination and reformulation of key words and constructions in contemporary logic. They attacked the isolation of "real" objects from "minds," of "words" from the speaker, of "knowings" from the "known." They also emphasized the central importance of viewing persons and objects against the perspective of the transactions or processes of change and action within society and physical nature.

In 1954, at the age of eighty-four, Bentley brought out a volume of his essays, appropriately called *Inquiry Into Inquiries.* Three years later a noted group of Bentley's admirers published a volume in his honor, *Life, Language, Law,* under the editorship of Richard Taylor. That same year, on May 21, Bentley died. His influence in opening new vistas is stronger now than in most of his lifetime. In 1964 the Rutgers University Press published *John Dewey and Arthur F. Bentley: A Philosophical Correspondence, 1932–1951,* which attracted wide attention. The Syracuse University Press will publish within the near future Bentley's *Makers, Users, and Masters.* And the appearance of *A Great Society?* this year indicates that the ideas of Bentley can still move men to debate, to fresh insights, and to joint action for the welfare of the diverse groups that constitute "man-society."

# INTRODUCTION

In 1908 I published a volume, *The Process of Government*, to which I refer for illustration of the practical use of the attitude of investigation herein made explicit. That attitude was in a small way one of relativity in the statement of all social facts, though, of course, without knowledge or use of the term which has now become so significant for all science. It recognized no fundamental man, and no society assumed as somewhere external to the individual man, but strove to describe and interpret the processes of government and public opinion in terms of group activities, taken each—as we would now put it—in relativity to the others.

Much that was vague, troublesome and difficult in the investigation of society when that book was written has become clear and patently reasonable since Minkowski made space and time commensurable dimensions, and since Einstein discovered that there might be many differing systems of space and of time—that is, of the extensions of the experienced world—without any one of these systems having, so far as our present knowledge is able to go, any priority, any claim to be fundamental to the others.

These discoveries, combined with those concerning the action of the electrons inside the atoms,—"inside" being in this respect an almost meaningless term, but the best verbal indicator at the moment available—and combined with the progressive resolution of the old verbal monstrosities of psychology by the logicians, pragmatists and behaviorists, have set us free—we may at least hope—to envisage social facts, not as verbal dummies supported on creaking frameworks of similar dummies, but in terms and with understanding which will give sound functioning results in study.

Physics has frankly admitted that its deepest truths are phases of functioning human knowledge and not exterior dominators of knowledge. The split of matter and mind, formerly posited as fundamental, is no longer before us in any sense that need interfere with unified scientific study. Mass no longer sits blunt and solid but has become a variable factor of action, in knowledge. Existence, as something definable for any instant, without past or present, has no longer its old deadening effect. "Action at a distance" is no longer assumed by the physicist even for gravitation, and the old psychol-

ogies will profit. Space as a barrier, sharply dividing one man from another and demanding that we
make a separate unit out of each, has lost its hurtful
power. Time has secured a unifying, not a splitting,
meaning. Man's society, without the unworkable
structures of mass and space and time and hope-
lessly concreted individuals, can now begin to be
interpreted.

The reason for dividing so short an essay as this
into three formal parts is because of the very different
degrees of authority which the different portions of
the treatment possess. The first part is descriptive
and, at that, descriptive only of the values which
the new physics has as a background for a study
of man and society. I am not so presumptuous as
to attempt exact statement of Einstein's results,
but am concerned rather with the value for my
science of that attitude towards the physical world
for which Einstein's name is the label, and which is
common not only to him and his followers but to his
progressive critics.

The second part, described as "limitations" pretends to no importance save in the one respect alone
which makes it necessary here, that of guarding
against the many misconceptions which old hardened
terms of practical every-day life drag in as we use
them, without our recognizing what they are doing to

us, and often against our will when we do have some recognition of it.

The third part alone endeavors to attain proper exactness in a field with which the writer has done his best to become familiar. The attempt at exactness is made with the use of not to exceed half a dozen terms in specialized meanings, and these held as close to common usage as possible: although it has long been evident that progress in detail here will require a large technical vocabulary, as it does in every other region of science. Words are our most essential tools: if they are not exact they cease to be tools for our service and quickly become instruments for our destruction.

.  .  .  .  .  .  .

This manuscript was finished as it stands, except for a few added notes, and the afterword, in the spring of 1924. Personal disability has prevented attention to its publication until the present. Re-reading it, I am led to one or two further observations.

Were I writing today I would give a more direct treatment, one structurally more prominent, to the psychological and cultural descriptive approaches to the whole body of material, by way of showing that neither treatment can be regarded as an addition to the other, but that either is susceptible of extension over all of the material. Both have their uses, but those uses do not include determinations of causation as between them. I would assert and develop directly the assertion that within any given mass of observations, of any kind of material, at any stage whatever of the development of those observations from crudity to eloquence or to systematization, the psychic cannot be picked out clean from the cultural, nor the cultural clean from the psychic; the curves being open at both ends. I would have no hesitation in undertaking to follow this argument down as acutely as possible in any field whatever, where the goal in question is a proof that interpretation must be within the joint system, and not from one form of statement to the other.

I feel also the need of one further word of explanation as to the manner of treatment given to physical relativity in the text. My approach is not from the position of the sociologist who, to his own large body of knowledge, has added no doubt in every case as much of understanding of recent developments in physics as is here utilized. Nor is it, of course, from the point of view of physics or any of the natural sciences, to use the old, but now almost meaningless term. The approach is, instead, from the great background of common and every-day practice, knowledge and formulation of knowledge in the naïve definitions of the dictionaries, within the range of which the sociologies do their work. And since it is this whole background and all the formulations of it which are already witnessing the beginnings of reconstruction under the influence of relativity, it is incumbent on me to make clear the nature of that reconstruction as I see it and as it influences my own work. So I may apologize to the physicist for what he will doubtless think a very peculiar way of discussing relativity and to the sociologist for restating much of his own extra-professional information, and nevertheless feel that without myself going over this field in my own way I could not advance towards any degree of intelligibility in the theoretical positions I take.

Despite some question as to its advisability, I am holding to my original plan of letting my text run without encumbrance of detail, and throwing all comment and reference into a later section of the book. This later section therefore covers the field of the text in a disjointed way with illustration, criticism and reference. Any reader personally concerned with the problems in question will use the two treatments jointly as may best fit his needs.

I wish to express my thanks to my friends, Professor Richard P. Baker, of the University of Iowa, and Dr. Sinclair Smith, of Mt. Wilson Observatory, for their kindness and valuable assistance in reading both my manuscript and proof sheets; but, of course, without holding them in any way responsible for my own inadequacies, or perhaps sometimes deliberate superficialities of statement, in the fields in which such methods of statement are ungrateful to them.

ARTHUR F. BENTLEY.

# CONTENTS

# Contents

# Contents

# Contents

# Contents

# Relativity in Man and Society

---

## PART I

## THE MEANING OF RELATIVITY

### Description

# I

## Man, Society and Einstein

In ordinary description man and society, since Einstein announced his discoveries, have undergone little change that may be definitely attributed to him. Developing processes in evidence before have been continuing without measurable shunting or acceleration, though to what is called the history of ideas an important addition has been made.

Einstein's results, however, are now a part of human knowledge: not final knowledge—knowledge is never that—but developing, working knowledge. Man and society, in any meanings these words are entitled to have, are also a part of that knowledge, and sharers in its development, though it is they at the same time who present themselves as its bearers. And it so happens that by transforming physics, the Einstein results have taken steps which are to prove of the greatest importance in transforming knowledge of society. The two fields are on a simpler meeting ground than they have ever been before.

The meaning of Relativity, identified so largely with the name Einstein, which we have now to examine is not what Einstein himself means by his results, nor what the present writer or any other writer thinks he means or ought to mean. It is not a judgment on the minute changes which his calculations have made in the measured statement of a few sidereal facts. It has not to do with the "curvature" or "warping" of space, nor with any other of the spectacular phrasings of journalism. It is a very complex phenomenon to be approached from many sides.

It concerns itself not only with Einstein's writings, but with those of the other investigators in series behind and after him, with his constructive critics as well as with his personal followers, with a direct effect on the reconstruction of technical language—where, indeed, most spectacular "curvatures" and "warpings" are now seen to be located, and with a further effect on the reconstruction of all speech and thought in the other fields, notably that of society, where its achievements apply. It is a social meaning both as to its origins and its effects. Its pasts and its futures are both involved in its definition. It is itself an affair of relativity at the same time that relativity is the key-word of its subject matter.

"Man" and "Society" and "Einstein" are not three definite subjects "about" which we may make remarks, and "between" which we may establish relations. They are before us first of all as words. They are rough practical words which point vaguely at fields of study. They are very suspicious words. Define Einstein to the limit of our ingenuity as a man, and we have made no progress, rather the reverse, towards defining Einstein as a phenomenon of society.

## II

### The Term "Einstein"—Its Meanings

Who, first of all, is Einstein, the man? A German, a Jew, long an engineer in the Swiss patent office, more recently a university professor with family and regular meals, with friends around him, with birth behind and death ahead, and with a few brief writings to his credit, some of which of but a few pages have made the whole fraternity of mathematicians and physicists whirl with a new intense activity, bearer of a name which the best opinion today believes will remain in human memory coupled with Copernicus and Galileo and Newton as a pathfinder of the universe. Has he a brain of exceptional fineness and power within the bone of his skull? We do not know. Physiologists and anthropologists may speculate on this a little within limits, but with no certain confidence.

But what do we imply by the term Einstein if we wish to speak of the status of man and of society since Relativity, since Einstein? We mean a statement, an attitude, a position towards the physical world, specified definitely and exactly for physicists and mathematicians, and in a way leading to spectacular features in common knowledge, by the activity of the man Einstein. We mean this statement or attitude, not as a cold "thing," self-existent, as the term goes, but as a value for us, as a functioning part of the knowledge and of the life of today. When we say Einstein we have in mind an achievement of the very greatest importance in our handling of the physical world today—first in our knowledge-attitude towards that world, more definitely in our computations of the greatest and smallest measurements of that world, and last in what will come out of it for all of us in our control of that world. And to this we shall have to add its value for all of that world we contrast with the physical, which we refer to under terms of man and mind and society or other words whatsoever.

Taking, then, first the values for the physical world, on what rests the almost universal confidence that in Einstein we have immensely the best handling of that world we have ever had? The physicists and mathematicians—the comparatively few of them who have as yet gained working mastery of the difficult tensor analysis that Einstein used—

speak of the "beauty" of his work, its orderliness, the perfection of its parts, the perfection and neatness of its relations with the rest of their knowledge. But this alone does not decide them in their knowledge. It is that the theory "works." It has worked in explaining a difficulty in their knowledge of the orbit of Mercury for which heretofore no explanation had been secured, despite most prolonged studies, which carried with it any satisfaction. It has worked in predicting a photographic displacement of the position of fixed stars, according as the light from them did or did not pass close to the sun in coming to us, that displacement being due to the gravitational effect of the sun on the light rays in their passage, and being in amount almost exactly what Einstein had calculated. It has worked in predicting a displacement of lines in the solar spectrum as compared with lines in the spectra of the same elements where the light has origin on earth, the verification here being partially, though not yet completely, established.

Let the question of confidence go with this. The meaning of Einstein, the value of him in this sense of physics, lies in a new and greater exactness in what was heretofore supposed to be the most exact, if not the only exact, possession men had acquired in all the history of their thought, and in the practical effects it is already beginning to have in the handling of the physical world.

But this meaning of Einstein, no matter how much one may elaborate it, letting it stand as a working attitude and announcement attached to the one man whom we have so briefly described as a man among men, is far from giving us a social statement of the phenomenon. Rather this meaning attaches to a group of men, coming only to definite comprehensive and spectacular statement in the man Einstein. To state it fully the meaning would have to be carried to the confines of human history: and could be rightfully so carried. For our purposes here, however, and considering the present restrictions of our knowledge, it is legitimate to limit the statement and the group to which we attach it, without setting any barrier to further extensions elsewhere for other purposes.

Taken socially in this way, then, the meaning of Einstein may be considered in a group of workers concerned with one weak point in the old geometry of Euclid and with one bitter fact which, when laid bare in exact and unmistakable simplicity, seemed in flat conflict with all other substantial measureable human experience.

The weak point in geometry had to do with parallel lines, and does not need attention here except in

what came out of it.   In trying to get it clear several
men about the middle of the last century tried what
would develop if they abandoned Euclid's axioms
and worked from opposed or different axioms.   Two
of these men, Gauss and Riemann built the geometry that Einstein later used.   It did not assume that the straight line is the shortest distance
between two points, nor that parallel lines never
meet, and it had the peculiarity that its reasonings
could be carried on without specified quantities, so
that in its broadest generalization it seemed to
handle qualities as well as quantities; and the
further peculiarity that it could be made to work
for four or five or more dimensions of space as
well as for the three dimensions of Euclid and of
our common language.   In this way a tool was
provided.

The bitter fact was established by Michelson at
Chicago in 1887, and verified repeatedly in the following decade by him and by others.   It was that
while all other velocities were treated as if they
compounded, the velocity of light could not be calculated in with the others.   Light would not compound. Its speed as measured by Michelson's instruments was exactly the same whether the light went
along with the earth in the same direction the earth
was going in space, or whether it went at right angles

to the earth's path.   No subtraction.   No addition.
Its own gait.

Men thought of this for years, and then an
Irishman, Fitzgerald, suggested that the trouble
might not be with light, but that instead the trouble
might be with the measuring tools, that perhaps
the high speed at which the earth was going made
these tools themselves shrink or flatten out against
that speed, but not crossways to it.   Perhaps everything flattened out in the direction of motion at
high speeds, the tools included.

Next a Hollander, Lorentz, computed exactly the
amount of flattening that would be necessary to
explain the Michelson experiments.   That is, he established a formula containing symbols for the various factors, upon the basis of which one could calculate the flattening at any given speed.   His work
was sound: his formula is now an accepted one, so
far as it goes: but not in the background he had
in mind for it, not as indicating a shrinkage of
things that were unshrunk before they took on
such speed.

Here Einstein produced the first part of his theory,
that of special relativity as he calls it.   In the field
of motions not interfered with by other motions (mechanics, omitting gravitation) he proved that nothing need be regarded as shrinking from an actual one

size to an actual another size, but that everything
took its size, in our knowledge, in accordance with
relative speeds of the observer and the thing observed: that we had no grounds for saying that
one size (for example that size which is measured
under normal conditions on earth) was correct and
that another size was a shrinkage or deviation
from that correct size, but that our normal earth
size itself, as well as all other size relations,
was dependent on the squint from which it was
caught.

He proved it.  That means nothing more, and
nothing less, than that he established to the satisfaction of practically all trained judges of such matters, that his statements and his formulas agreed
better with observations of fact than the previous
statements and formulas had agreed.

Next came a Russian, Minkowski.  Working on
different lines with the geometry of Riemann he
showed that one of those possible additional dimensions of geometry which Riemann provided was
really known to us, that it was time, as we knew it,
that fitted into this geometry as a fourth dimension;
and he proclaimed that space and time were one
continuous whole, that the old distinction between
the words space and time, had only such validity as
the earlier distinction between height and width and

length, that we knew no space existence apart from time, no time existence apart from space, but only space-time as one unified setting.

Then came Einstein again, with his general relativity, his later theory in which gravitation is brought into the system. Gravitation, the laws of which had been worked out to a very close approximation by Newton, but which had always remained the maverick of physics, a lone Force, which seemed to "work at a distance": this gravitation was given more exact laws than it had had before, more exact because the new formulas enabled us to compute more exactly the observable facts—and what is much more important for our purposes, it was brought by Einstein back into the fold of our knowledge of nature along with the rest of physical facts, made a special case of that difference of measurement which occurs with different velocities of observation, given its statement in space-time, became in fact along with all other knowledge part of the life of the observer. Again, not as a dream, or rapt vision, not as speculation or philosophy, but as demonstrable knowledge, interpreting, measuring, and in the end predicting experience.

Two Germans, an American, an Irishman, a Hollander, a Russian and again a German. These are the human attachments, within our present limited range, of the term Einstein, as we commonly use his name with scientific reference.

And now came 1919 and the observations of the eclipse of the sun. Suddenly the world of newspapers and periodicals and the reading public rang with the overthrow of Newton, the warping of space, the vanishing of size, and other spectacular tales. Here arose at once another and very different value for the term Einstein. Instead of a value for a specialized group of workers extending over the investigations of a dozen men more or less, it became a very wide spread, popular term for a series of curiosities involving their every-day speech, and especially for that speech as interpreter of realities, themselves part of that speech. Crudely approximative, when viewed by the specialist, this value is nevertheless one that will develop in the next generation a change of meanings and understandings and attitudes in every-day life as significant as those earlier changes when the flat earth became round, and the centering of the heavens around the earth changed to the drifting of an earth speck in infinite space.

And beyond this there is still another value for the term, which is already beginning to unfold itself in what we are to know about ourselves in society. From the remodelling of the common language, as affected by the technical reconstruction of a few special terms in it, is beginning to arise a reconstruction of all technical knowledge of society and of man operating in society. Not through the mastery of a powerful calculus, but with qualitative rearrangements of our knowledge much less certain and reliable, but the best we yet have, will this work proceed.

Einstein, the man, his own theoretical positions, the group of similar workers for which his name is a label, their system of thought, a popular application to crude common understandings, the beginnings of reconstruction of all knowledge of man's life and activity, these are values for the term Einstein, knitted together, and running even farther, if it was in our field to trace them. If we could fully interpret Einstein in terms of what is called the history of thought we would have made a long step. But such an interpretation is no sooner begun than it leads back into human activities much fuller and richer than the word "thought" conveys. And interpretation here, despite its rich promise is beyond our present powers to carry through. To indicate the path towards it is our problem. We have next to locate certain phases of the scientific meaning of the term Einstein, which have peculiar value for such problems as this and for all our knowledge of society.

## III

### Relativity in Physics

Probably there is no man, not even some one most notoriously obstinate in his opinions, who will not occasionally admit that there may be two points of view upon some topic of discussion. If he will not admit it as to any topic upon which he himself has taken a flat stand, he will at least admit it where the issue is drawn between two other persons. Thus a full page advertisement of a patent medicine may be "good" from the point of view of expanding business, "bad" from some particular point of view about the patent medicine habit. Or again some huge gift to charity may appear to one man as a benevolence, to another as a gesture of display, to a third as a sop to conscience. In these illustrations we see the substance, in a floating field of superficial opinion, of what is meant by relativity. It is closely connected with the limited meanings of the current terms of language, no one of which covers adequately the phenomenon it is trying to characterize. The over-opinionated man is in fact an idolater of his own words.

Relativity in physics is a special case of this very general use of the term; with, however, a huge difference in importance. It has to do primarily with motion, then with space, time and energy, with gravitation and electricity. It has to do with fields of the most accurate measurement men have yet found themselves capable of. Its revisions of meaning are carried through in the most accurate language men possess, that of mathematics. It proves itself in the most exact prediction and practice. Its results are so fundamental that they are forcing revisions of meaning in all language, in all knowledge and in all common background ideas of life and experience.

There are many ways of stating technically what physical relativity is. They seem so different to the layman that he must just trust to the physicist that they all come to the same thing in his broader vision. Let us try to picture what physical relativity means in terms of our own every-day relation to the space and time world around us. It is just a special case within that broadest of all characterizations which we may give to the progress of human knowledge, the passage from man as a center to man as a portion, a passage which, strangely enough, is not degrading man to a detail, but instead raising him—these are poor words, but the best we have—to comprehensiveness.

Our generation and several generations before us have been brought up in a fairly definite attitude towards space and time, using words with fairly accurate practical meanings and relegating the hard problems to a separate word, infinity, which we sometimes ponder over, but usually rest content with ignoring. We are on a spherical earth, that earth is revolving around the sun, the sun itself is moving in some way with respect to the stars, the stars are spread out enormously in space and again enormously in time; space and time are real, they are there, destroy their contents and they would still be there, they are infinite, space in all directions, time backwards and forwards. We make these statements as though we understood them, and only with the word infinite do we commonly admit we do not know what we mean: we cannot consistently think boundaries to real space and real time, for their very essence to us is their continuing, so we just call them infinite to indicate that quality, and proceed about our business.

So much for our generation. It has not always been this way in the common attitude of men, thinking in their word systems, and it cannot be this way much longer. Since Einstein the world has found out too much for this to continue.

Go back not so very far into human history, and it was also different. The world in the first place was flat. Ignoring the hills and valleys on which you travelled, it spread out right and left and forward and behind. It went down deep enough to be solid to stand on and build on, and up high enough to keep its clouds and stars out of your grasp. Somewhere on a very high mountain sat the gods. Of course the world had boundaries, that was natural. What was across the boundaries need not bother you. The world went back a way in time—you had some views as to who started it. It was going to continue a way in time,—and you had some views as to what would end it.

By and by the earth ceased to be flat and became round. There were some interpretations of experience, some theories, and of course some men killed for them, and then came proofs of roundness by travelling around and finally still better proofs than these, coming from the use of physical and mathematical tools. That settled the business of limits to space so far as the surface of the globe was concerned. The surface of the earth no longer needed either boundaries or infinity: it simply wasn't built so as to need them.

By and by the sun and stars ceased in common opinion to revolve around the earth, simply because men had come to know too much about them to deal with them in that way. Ptolemy's system with its cycles and epicycles became too complicated to hold the full content of observations. Copernicus showed a simpler system with the planets revolving around the sun. Bruno abandoned the heliocentric theory and placed the sun among the stars. Kepler determined the elliptic orbits of the planets. Galileo developed a mechanics of motions on earth. Newton put the earth mechanics, gravitations and the siderial and planetary motions together in one system. The thing was done—for a while. Predictions were possible which led to discoveries; common meanings of words, common attitudes towards the physical world around, changed and adapted themselves to experience.

In a broad sense all of this was a development of relativity. Experiences that had been separate were brought into relation to one another and given their values and meanings in terms of one another.

But Newton bequeathed to us an absolute space and an absolute time. His relativity required him to postulate them. His principles would not work without them. And yet he did not use them. They were the verbal setting for his achievements. It was all in terms of matter, the inertia of matter, which was mass, and the motions of matter in space and time in exact calculable ratios. He left us another extraneous factor, also. This was Force. Gravitation acted in accordance with mechanical formulas but it acted at a distance. It required a postulate of Force to make up for lack of contact.

So long as all was matter and motion, things went very well for the physicist. He had his outlying verbal bothers, but he got along without solving them. And then entered the electro-magnetic phenomena, and the development of their laws, their working formulas, by Clerk-Maxwell. There were also the laws of light and radiation. For them the physicists formed another word, Ether, as a location in which to place their new facts:—ether supposed to surround and permeate matter, and fill space. Another puzzle word, but necessary as a background; so it seemed to the physicists, if physics was to be held together into one system.

Comes Einstein's relativity and holds things together in one scientific system, not by positing these verbal puzzle-backgrounds, space and time and force, and ether, but by getting in behind the various working formulas, and showing the condition under which certain new formulas will work out into all of them. The Newtonian law of gravitation needed revision in this way, leaving Newton's law as one special case of the new law.    The laws of electro-magnetic phenomena were taken over merely by restating them.

As relativity, how does this fit into the long historical series?    It is by introducing the observer's position, by showing how what is one record for one observer may be a different record for another. And under what special condition as to the observer? Under the condition, namely, that the observers are themselves moving at different velocities.    At the low velocities the differences are not noticeable or recordable.    They seem to take place in a fixed space and time.    At the high velocities the differences became significant, and they tear out that fixed space and time when they are harmonized. There is nothing left of that space and time, as existent itself, as a conditioning mould in which all happens.    It itself varies with the observations which alone show it at all.    It varies in its measurements, so that if you still assume it, it must be as something that is one thing at one time and another thing at another time, or in short just nothing at all. The process seems fearfully destructive, but nothing is destroyed but a word, a bad word, a puzzle word.

Under Newton relativity meant that the velocity of one point with reference to any other point could always be exactly determined.    He discarded all

efforts at determining absolute velocities, but held
that within an absolute space and time the relative
velocities could be determined.

Under Einstein relativity means that these velocities drag their space and time with them, that no
one of the spaces and times has any exactness of
determination except by taking into account the
velocity of the observation from which it is determined, that no one of them has more authority than
any other, that each has meaning only in terms
of others.

The cosmos of man from a little practical range
of definite objects of his activity, became a great
swinging system in which he found himself involved
as an insignificant speck, and now again its very
greatnesses and littlenesses are involved in his own
participation in the swing, so far as he can be defined in his own velocities relative to the others.
He has found a trick in the words he has been using
about his most dependable experiences, those of
space and time.  He has not indeed freed himself
yet from the tricks of his own language, but, in a last
resort, he has at least gained a knowledge of the
kind of trick those words are playing so as to be
better on his guard.

What is true under relativity as to the space and
time of the old physics and the old common under-

standing is true also as to other fundamentals of the
old physics.   Mass in physics which since Newton
has been the definite characteristic of all matter,
and assumed as indestructible, proves now to be
variable with velocity, and, besides being a measure
of inertia, has a definite value in terms of energy.
Mass can now be thought of as a form of energy.

Return now from man as the center of his cosmos
to man as the center of his relations with other men.
If his most stable words, space and time, have
crumpled under his hands, and proved to be variable factors in his experience, how much more will
the same probably prove to be true with the vague
and passing words which he used to denote his relations in his societies.   There has been a long development, a loosening and freeing of his idea and
opinion systems in his social life akin to what he
has had in his cosmos.   Can it strike down still
further?   In place of a relativity allowing for pre-
judice and error and position, can it strike down to
a relativity that abandons not only the certainty
of this or that opinion in favor of some possible
other, but the certainty of all except in terms of
others, except in terms of the purposive activities
of social living out of which they spring?   The
tendency of scientific thought in other lines of investigation besides those of physics is in this direction.

That it will advance from the stage of possibility to that of practical certainty seems to be indicated by the fundamental accomplishments in the field of physics.

# IV

## Space

Space is a problem of language. Language is a tool of living. It is a development of communication, and communication even in its simplest form involves more than one communicant. Language including every word in it is social, an activity of more than one. All the living that involves language is social living. Languages developed as we know them have meaning only in terms of billions of men spread in time and space: while time and space and the men themselves and the billions counted are only contents of language. All the splits of meaning, all the bifurcations, as they have been called, are within language, or within knowledge or within society, in whichever way we may choose to characterize them.

To talk of space except in terms of words, would be admitted as impossible under any definition of talk and words. To think of space except in terms of words is equally impossible. Try it if you think you can think of it without words. Leave out the words, and you have left only a stoppage, a state of suspense. You are satisfied—or drugged—if you can fit some words together. You are puzzled if your words will not work—and quit in confusion. Your success depends on how well your words function with—fit into—other words. Throw up a dead word—dead because it pretends to indicate something outside of words, outside of thought, outside of society—a clot, a clod, a lump—and you are done, except perhaps for obstinacy, which in the last resource is stupidity.

It has come to pass that for the physical world the best language, the best thought, the best understanding, is mathematics, once a structure of spatial and temporal mensuration, generalized in numbers, which were still quantities, now generalized still further, not into qualities so far as quality contrasts with quantity, but into what may be called characteristics, susceptible of quantitative determination on one side, and giving more than a hint of a coming qualitative determination on the other.

The task of popular language, popular thought, popular conception of the cosmos is now to take over in common terms for daily use the more exact knowledge offered by the mathematical language of the new physics. It seems difficult but it is not. True it cannot be done in a moment. One requires a little time to adapt one's self. But break a tough word or two, and the result for popular thought will be simplification and comparative ease.

You go forward or backward, right or left and up or down. You can split the angles in any way. For every forward and backward you have your rights and lefts and ups and downs. Rights and lefts are evidently relative to forward and backs, but ups and downs seem more positive. Yet you know that if you go to the opposite side of the earth up and down will reverse with each other.

You rely on measuring rods, but you have long known that for delicate work measuring rods change with heat. Now you must add the fact that for still more delicate work they change with velocity.

You have been taught a theory of straight lines, but you know you never experienced anything more than an approximation to one. You know that if you follow the straightest line you can across the surface of the earth you will come back to your starting point—you will have been follow- ing a circle. The one straight line you really know anything about is the path of a ray of light. It is here, it is there, 186,000 miles a second, and straight- ness is its path. But it too goes astray. As you curve unwittingly going around the earth, so it curves as it passes close to the sun. The photographic plate, deadly tell-tale, shows its origin, the star it comes from, in one position relative to neighbor stars, when our sun, under eclipse so we can catch the beam, is close to its path, and in another position relative to its neighbors on the plate, when our sun is far away.

Was it straight in one course, and was it curved in another? That is a matter of the words you use. It is always the straightest thing you know, that ray of light. Cleave to the straight the first time, and it is curved the second. Cleave to the straight the second time and it is curved the first. But by what right cleave to either? Better revise your words. Go straight or go in curves, practically, as you will on the surface of the earth and in your dealings with its materials. But do not take your oath on either straightness or curvature beyond your experience, and beyond the experience of the specialists who represent you in your more difficult dealings with experience; your architects, your engineers, your astronomers, your physicists, your mathematicians. That is not hard. Simply loosen up the two tough words, and admit openly at last that they have never been anything but sops to your troubles of thought.

Are your words straightness and curvature made fit for the wider experience, you have little more difficulty with space. It helps you nothing to make a banner out of the word and wave it, to hurrah for it, exalt it, swear by it. If you cannot rely on it to be straight the same way twice you cannot rely on it at all, as an absolute word, an outside lump fact. Take it for what it is. You will go just as straight practically as ever; you will have just as much space in which to live and experience and act, but you will cease to let a bad definition claim a power it no longer is entitled to, even hypothetically.

Let Einstein and his fellows compute the curvatures and the humps in huge spatial experiences, let them calculate the possibilities of such spatial experience rounding back into itself comparable to the surface of a sphere as we know it, let them compute the mass of all spatial contents, let them revise their formulas, supersede their closest statements of the present with better statements of the future, just as those have superseded the formulations of Newton, turning Newton's laws into special cases of more general laws. The physicists are your representatives in this work. But hold fast to this achievement. The absolute space that Newton found it necessary to posit, but could not use, and that we have retained as a common meaning of existence, has now been studied and used, and is no longer the tough word, the absolute space, but a flexible form of experience under our hands, subject to such meaning practically and scientifically as each experience when fully enough studied gives to it.

Face a flat and very thin wall. Walk around it at a distance and it disappears from sight. It exists for you in space because you walk still further around and again control the other side and have it control you in your action, if perchance you try to walk through it. You are used to this. But it is no more crushing to know that if the wall were replaced by a cube and if the cube flew by you with the speed of light, and if you had competent instruments to measure its length as it flew by—replacing with such instruments your eyes which are competent only for very small speeds, not high ones—your instruments would show that its length had disappeared in the direction of its motion. You do not have a shrinkage in a real space—you have instead a better understanding of space as a word applicable to your experience, for the measuring process is experience—just so far as it fits and no further.

There is still another battling ground for our old

word space.   It lies inside the atom where wonderful skill in measurement has caught the electrons in their motion, computed their speeds, established their orbits to some extent, shown that they were limited as to what particular orbits they might occupy out of a possible very large number, and where further—as the case stands today—they seem, when they change from one orbit to another, to leave the one and appear in the other without intervening steps which mathematics can at present recognize; and moreover to need computation not in terms of step by step around the orbit, but in some way in terms of whole orbits as units.   Much of this is uncertain and vague, and the fascinating work is being pushed with great power.   For us it means only this.   Should the electrons in their orbits prove to follow the indicated laws, being now here, now there—a definite there, but with no between—another assault on the clotted uses of the word space would have been made.   The space effect would be, one might say, built up seemingly out of what was not space.   And should they require computation in terms of whole orbits, not steps around an orbit, the space meaning would become very different again from what it has been in our recent current language and thought.

# V

## Time

The exact instantaneous simultaneous happening of two events in different space locations is practically assumed in every-day life, but cannot be proved as fact any more than the straightness of a line, in any arbitrary definition of straightness. The current popular thought of time as a "now" that exists, with a "past" that is real and yet no longer exists, and a "future" that is real and yet has not yet come into existence, and with problematic extensions where we cannot follow it indicated by the sense defying word infinity, has turned out to be an error, a bad use of a word.

What has been said about the wordiness of space applies also to the word time.

Vision is not our only sense. If it were not for active tactile sensation or other helps to vision we would not know solid bodies, would not know a three dimensional world, we would not say that it exists.

Or, at least, if we could know these things we do not know what the process of our knowledge would be.    It would be by some process beyond our present explanation.

We know how faulty and incomplete are our senses—we even know that other living beings besides man on this earth have senses keener in some aspects and possibly other senses different in quality.    We correct the imperfections of each sense by the others, eye by ear or touch or taste or smell, and so around.    We correct all the sense returns by the use of tools, and by more and more delicate instruments, most delicate and exact of all instruments being mathematics.

If then we squat solidly on our present popular use of words and say that the world exists in time at this moment in just the particular way we have been accustomed to use in defining our words, and no other; and that a while ago it existed somewhat differently, but that that is over forever: while later on it will exist still differently but that such existence has not begun yet, are we not very stupidly and obtusely tying ourselves to nothing more substantial than an uncorrected report of our senses and a very imperfect and approximate definition of words?

Twenty-five years ago a critical query such as

the above could have been the prelude to nothing better than speculations and dreams, very fascinating to those whom they interested, entirely justified in their range as speculations, but of no other authority. Today they express a real requirement imposed upon us by the finer development of our sense achievements which our tools have given us.

It is not difficult to grasp time in the new sense—less difficult even than to grasp space—providing as before we waive our idolatry of language, of words we are accustomed to in meanings which only satisfy us as refuges from thought. Some bits of every-day knowledge will help us.

In the first place psychological time, which most of us have in mind when we use the term, is not the same as sidereal time, which astronomers and mathematicians use. One is a fleshly judgment. The other is an affair of the accuracy of clocks. Starting with our fleshly judgments, we know how they differ in estimating durations in quiet times from times of great excitement. Compare our waking durations with those of dreams. In a few seconds of waking moment we may dream durations of hours or days. And on the other hand in estimating elapsed time—what o'clock it is—we are generally more accurate in periods covered by sleep than by waking hours. It is a very confused report we get from psychological time, with a greater, but still very remote, approximation to clock time, the smaller the content of experience or the more routine-like the experience.

Some card players are better than others because of what we call their memory. But memory happens to be only a word, with a meaning about which psychologists are much less confident than are laymen in everyday use. What the better card player seems to have is more of the game before his attention at each moment. It is only our common interpretation that splits up the facts, causing us to say that we remember "this" (past), and foresee "that" (future), and are doing "this other" (present).

A phenomenal chess player, we have reason to believe, is one who with more delicate and complex structure in some regions of his brain, visualizes the game as a whole. The first few moves present to him whole complexes of moves. And when he can carry on many games at once he must have these realities of action in periods of time—not as mere present instants with separate remembered pasts and separate anticipated futures—much more vividly still before him as wholes.

Oriental races with what we call ancestor worship have perhaps underlying this worship a more vivid grasp of durations of human history as realities in time than Occidentals have ever had.

Psychologists are inclined to think that a dog does not get a three dimensioned space world as men get it, but that as he goes racing along the road or through the woods he has something better described as two space dimensions and one time dimension, not of course time as we are now called to grasp it along with our three space dimensions; but a world built of planes or flat spaces, running in time.

It comes to this. We must revise our word time which we have taken to be an instantaneous present, with on the one hand memory of something past and on the other with a forward look, and make the word mean for us an extension of existence just as real as any extension in space—just as real that is, in its backward and forward directions, as is space in its backward and forward, right and left and up and down directions. From our old popular definition or understanding of space we have taken off something because it cannot keep its straightness at a fine test. To our old popular understanding of time we must add something because its instantaneousness and its simultaneity are not enough for it. Space dimensions and the time dimension come to a common denominator in our experience.

And now why?

A physicist does not know anything instantaneous. He can reduce his time coordinate to zero as a limit. But he is then not dealing with physics. Euclidean geometry never pretended to be physics —it was mathematics, in the days when the two were separate. It is now a limiting case of a larger geometry. Take an assumed instantaneous section of life. From it you would not get a picture of society nor men, nor body cells, nor molecules, nor atoms, nor even electrons, though that is the last word we may use today in getting down to the instantaneous; for even the electrons are in violent motion in time with changing mass. As found they have duration. One must pass beyond all present indications of physics before getting to anything instantaneous. The photograph of the instantaneous would be blank, so far as present knowledge goes.

Simultaneity. One might say that if there was nothing known instantaneously there could be nothing assured simultaneously and be done with it. Our acquired knowledge, however, works the other way round. All that is said about the instantaneous is that the physicists have not found it. They have, however, proved the insecurity of our old definitions of simultaneity. If measurements of space and measurements of time, distances and durations, vary with the relative speeds of observer and event, the measurements will not be the same from all observers' positions. More truly one might say that they will not be exactly the same from any two observers' positions. If light were instantaneous and if direct lines were straight in the old sense, this would not be true. But light has a definite velocity, and this velocity will not compound with other velocities. We come to a point therefore where the "is" in time of one observer which differs from the "is" of another observer cannot be referred to any truer "is" for a final test. Each must stand as true as the other. The mathematician therefore plots us a diagram which roughly indicates to us a region of a past for all observers and another region of a future for all observers, but with another region in between which is past for some and future for others. And in this last region the simultaneous is lost and becomes meaningless, for what is past for the one will be future for the other and not the same for either. And even in the general pasts and futures, any particular point will have different time measurements for one of us than for others.

Durations remain to us with their pasts and presents, but not with the same definitions of past and present from all points of view, and with no test of rightness as between the varying definitions. We have a substantial time from earlys to lates, knitted up and inseparable. We must take it as such. It is a whole for us—a whole of experience—divided into distances and durations for purposes of study: capable of statement, so far as we know now, not as a whole, but in its relations of parts: but posited as a whole, so far as that gives us satisfaction: and finding its unity—if indeed there is a sense of the word unity which will ultimately apply to it—in human experience, which is society, again a term for examination which is at present before us rather as a point of approach, than as anything in the nature of an explanation or even provisional statement.

Reverting to rough indications of the reality as existence of past and present one may think of what the psycho-analyst digs out of early life experience from what he calls the unconscious to interpret what he calls the conscious. Amid all his vagaries and sensationalisms he does real work. Twenty-five years ago we would have been satisfied with a neurological present to explain to ourselves these results if we did not perhaps prefer some mystical or other-worldly statement. Today no. We must take it in durations, with no right to attribute an immediate reality to a very short one over a very long one, save as it is useful as a tool or method in our study.

And again, the whole evolutionary spread of the cosmos and of life on the globe gives us a reality of past and future in present in such a way that no arbitrary sharply defined present can be found. All is a net of pasts and futures, with the present only such particular duration, itself including within itself a stretch of small past-future, as we may choose to single out for examination. The "germ" of the future is not a figure of speech alone. The egg and the fowl and the recapitulation between them have values beyond those of a statement in naïve time alone.

That this freeing of our thought from bad and unworkable definitions of space and time is of vital importance in the study of society we shall see later. Until we can set before ourselves a fact that is typically social, so stated as to carry its social quality in the statement, we can make little progress. If our social fact is thought of as the present instant, it is hampered by a technique of relating to it past and future facts under some type of causation implied by them. But from now on we are justified, not only by our own observation, but by the achievements of physics and mathematics in picking our durations to conform with our problems, and in discarding the instantaneous and simultaneous. And similarly we are freed from the hampering of a dead space, the inability to hold combined as one fact something that to our cruder observation is separated by sections of a crude space background. We may take our facts in such space as they come in, knowing that from the electron to the most distant star cluster all the space is relative to the action.

Words, words, words. This chapter and the preceding are full of words which are bound to be subject to what we call misunderstandings. Each misunderstanding is really a function of some special definition or meaning of words habitual to a section or group of men in a defined historical and functional setting. In a few thousand words one cannot loosen up all the specialized meanings of these words. Against one particular misconception however a warning is necessary, at this point. To say that past and future have as great a reality as distance in space is of course not to say that they have a present reality in the sense of time alone. We have transcended that instantaneous type of present. Loosen up the word present from that definition in time, and they do have a present reality, again loosening the word reality to the meanings required.

Past and future stand before us as one in the sense of durations, from small durations to large: not as something mystical, not as something spectacular, but as the existence which is the field which scientific thought is working and developing. What comes out of it, the value of such a statement, is for work to show, and for that only.

# VI

## Space-Time: Action

In the preceding chapters the word reality has been repeatedly used in the sense of the world as it is laid before us in growing knowledge, or otherwise put, in increasingly accurate language. In this sense a passage of space reality from absolute to relative and of time reality from instantaneous or fictitious to relative has been described. Durations have been described as "present" and "real" just as much as distances.

A revision by combining the two relativities, time and space, is now necessary if the position of recent physics is to be adequately described. To the new physics what exists for study is not a field of space plus a field of time, but a single space-time continuum. One may perhaps put it something like this. In the discarded definitions of the words velocity involves time and space. But the measurements of both time and space, both durations and distances,

44

vary relatively to velocities, and these distances and durations comprise all that we know about time and space. Since the distances and durations vary relatively to each other in a common term, they are phases of a common experience or reality which for lack of other name is called space-time.

This apparently logical statement is not a proof. Its apparently logical form is merely an analysis and arrangement of words, but one that agrees well with the facts as they are now under study. The proof, if one wants that word, or better the fact, is that there is a definite quantity which mathematicians use, called the "interval," which enables them to handle measurements and make computations that agree with future happenings, when both distances and durations break up under their hands and prove variable and inaccurate. The interval is neither a rule nor a clock but their combined action. For any event that is studied the interval is invariant to all observers. It involves both its time and its space relations, and while no two observers at different velocities, can measure either the time or the space alike, all observers at whatever velocities measure the interval exactly alike. The interval involves both the time and the space relations of the event and is invariant while they vary. A rough attempt at picturing it is made by

Nordmann who compares it with the base of a triangle. No matter how the two other sides of the triangle vary in relative proportions according to the point at which the apex is located, the base remains the same. The sides would represent, in this attempted illustration, the relative time and space measures from different apex points and the base would represent the interval of the event invariant for all points of observation. Apart from any illustration, however, the fact that counts is, as has been said, that the interval is actually used by the physicists in making predictions that are more accurate than any ever made by the old uses of time and space. With the interval they have corrected the old laws of gravitation and removed conflicts of fact insoluble under the old physics of Newton.

The fact for physics is therefore thus far a velocity with the interval as its measuring rod. But that is not all. There is energy. There is mass. Mass and energy prove in the new physics to be different manifestations of the same thing. That is they are expressed by the same mathematical statements. Mass proves to vary with velocity just as time and space do. Lorentz prior to the Einstein results had calculated what variation there would be in the mass of matter if matter were electrical, that is if matter quantities acted the same way electrical quantities were known to act. When he figured the flattening of distance in the direction of motion at high velocities in an attempted explanation of the Michelson experiment, he secured the same ratios. And these same ratios prove themselves as to mass and energy in the new field of space-time.

The physicists have a word for this combined process though it is "combined" only from the point of view of the separation with which it was stated in the preceding paragraphs. Properly speaking the whole process is the primary fact they observe of which the duration, distance, energy and mass are measurements. The word is Action. Action is the event in the studied world, in combined terms of space and time and work, all varying with reference to one another.

Action is known in quantities, and not in any other way. Planck's quantum, which is revolutionizing knowledge of the electrons inside—as the word goes—the atom, is a measured unit of action. It is expressed in terms of work accomplished per second.

We have therefore a material of study, a type of fact, which is a living, moving process. Matter as something outside of action has no definition in physics and no need of definition or even of assump-

tion.   That which proceeds is what is studied, and
this procedure in the full measurement of the aspects
of its procedure, of its relations to other procedures,
is the field of physics.

Significant of the change is the adoption by physicists of the word "event" as it has been used several
times above.   Following the Einstein results, but
getting a different verbal approach certain men, as
Whitehead, have shown the aptness of this term
"event" to include phenomena commonly defined
in space alone as well as phenomena commonly
defined in time.   Minkowski had put his difficult
mathematical results in the simplest language thus:
"No one has ever seen a place other than in a
certain time, or a time other than in a certain place."
He had spoken of world-points, and world lines.
In short from the union of time and space he had
given us the event to consider.   A typical illustration would be the Washington monument.   Do we
think of it as an existing thing, as so much matter
that is there?   A glance at the full fact shows we
must revise that attitude.   The monument in its
planning, its foundation and partial construction,
its financial campaign, its completion, its weather-
ing and deterioration and repairs, its unending visit-
ation of citizens, stretching on into its termination or
replacement above ground, its foundation survivals

that may be examined by other races of men after
some new glacial era or submergence and emergence
of continents, from which much of its life history
can be read, perhaps on even till nothing but a soil
irregularity remains as a guide to interpretation,
is an event—the whole of it. It is analyzable into
series of events. It can be cut across in analysis
into many event sections, like planes through a
solid, each section taking some of the monument
aspect with much other aspect of life—as for example masonry technique or architectural technique,
or national symbolism or financial structure. But
every such event phase has duration. And if we
cut it down to the instantaneous—eliminate its
time phase, or as the mathematician says, make
its time coordinate zero, we then, and then only,
get to something that is unreal, not real. In an
assumed instantaneousness with space alone allowed as its form, it is not solid matter, not even
electrons, for instantaneous electrons are unknown
to physics or to any reality we may describe. It
would be beyond physics, and beyond any reality
we have to examine.

When we come in Part III to the direct discussion of society we shall find the phenomena it presents under the new world-aspect of action and
space-time much more amenable to investigation

than they have been heretofore in a background of unreal space and unreal time and unreal matter. Unreal dead space no longer will dominate our descriptions.   An unreal instantaneous present yields to a reality of durations permitting the full purposiveness of social process to receive unified description and treatment.

# VII

## Units and Limits

There remains to describe another aspect of the new physics as it has been developing under Einsteinian relativity. This has to do with the type of units and limits it presents. It has to do, we may perhaps say, with the dead spots, the verbal dead spots, in it, comparable in a way with the old deadnesses of infinity and absolute space and absolute time. Absolutes in a sense they still are, so far as their functioning goes, but no longer huge domineering absolutes, rather humble little absolutes securing no flustered acceptance, but forced to submit to a cold and hard scientific gaze.

Recall the passage of world attitude to the cosmos, from a world with boundaries through a world of infinity to a world of relativity. Once man measured the world by his reach, and added his neighbor's reach to his own, until just out of reach he placed a boundary. Then he put his world in a

space which he made infinite, without knowing
what he meant. Now he substitutes a space aspect
of experience which does not require either boun-
aries or infinity because it is merely a function of
what is happening.

But with all he has no pretense to "understanding" the universe as a whole process any more fully
than before. He has simply transferred his puzzles.
Now they fall in a region of numbers, relations of
one, two, three: and this realm of one, two, three,
the simplest of all matters perhaps to common sense,
is unfortunately, because of its very discreteness,
its one-two-threeness, one of the most difficult that
mathematicians have to work with and understand.

There are the fixities which may be compared
with the absolute zero long known to thermo-
dynamics, the point at which molecular motion
ceases. The limiting velocity of light, or some
velocity near it, which Einstein uses in his calcu-
lation, has repeatedly been referred to. There is
the volume of the universe, a subject on which
Einstein is continuing his work and which he believes can be satisfactorily measured. Eddington
suggests a relation between the volume of the universe and the radius of an electron. He also men-
tions the existence of a large pure number constant
approximating it at $3.10^{42}$. The actuality of the

interval as a measuring rod in space-time should be recalled in this connection.

There are now so many fixities in physics that books are sometimes published consisting of nothing but tabulations of them. Planck's constant is fundamental so far as present study of them goes. It is an elementary quantum of action measured as $6.54.10^{-27}$ erg. sec. which determines just how much energy an atom can radiate in any one process. This is not a guess, not a theory "up in the air." It is a fact for the knowledge of today on the basis of which the inner structure of the atom is investigated and coherently and rationally explained.

Rydberg's constant is a fundamental wave number which occurs in every study of spectral lines, 109,700 waves per centimeter. Divide this by $2^2$, $3^2$, $4^2$, $5^2$, and so forth and follow the other rules of procedure the physicists have developed, and the various series of spectral lines are worked out exactly as they prove to exist when measured.

Inside the atom the electrons revolve in orbits around their nuclei, and these orbits exist only at definitely fixed distances from the nuclei. They cannot be found at any possible distance but when the electron disappears from an orbit at one distance it reappears instantaneously, which merely means without measurable or calculable transition, in an orbit at another range. Not continuously, but units.

The table of chemical elements is now worked out with practically no gaps or doubtful spots in terms of the simple numerical series, one to ninety-two, with only four missing numbers in that series, but of course with an uncertainty how many numbers above ninety-two may exist or may yet be found.

The status of present physics could not be left without setting forth this situation. Needless to say there is at present no remark to be made relating this status to the study of society. If anybody believes that the individual man, such and such a clot of hands, feet, muscle cells and nerve cells, feelings and ideas, is such a unit, he is entirely free to prove it.

# PART II

# THE POSITION OF MAN

## Limitations

# VIII

## Inside and Outside: Far and Near

By way of transition from physics to man it is desirable to make a few remarks on the interesting little words, inside and outside, far and near. They are certainly simple enough. Every one of us assumes he knows all about them. And yet I am not risking very much in venturing the assertion that physics, which is our one branch of knowledge that really knows what it knows, does not know anything about them at all, has no place for them, no meaning for them, and would go ahead just exactly the same as it is going if those words, and everything connected with them were entirely removed from our language and knowledge.

We are in the habit for practical purposes of locating inside our bodies certain nutritive and neural processes. Our physiologists have progressively given these processes chemical and electrical interpretations; that is, as they have analyzed them they have displayed them in chemical and then in electrical terms.  So at length we have them before us to consider not in molecules and atoms, but in electrons.  This work has been partially accomplished and on such a basis as to make it the reasonable working hypothesis of the investigator that all of his material will ultimately be available for statement in such form.

Now while, as a matter of Euclidean space we still put the bread into our mouths, whence it passes to a further section of our insides, our stomachs, this Euclidean space in which this all happens is found to be only a partial approximation to the facts.  And when the bread in its electro-atomic action passes on into our bodily electro-atomic action we have the process going on under conditions in which the Euclidean space is most prominent for its gaps and its disappearances.  This is not satisfying to contemplate.  Our insides, it is true, have not become outsides, but they have nevertheless lost the distinguishing marks of their insideness.

And again we contemplate the bread we are about to eat and rejoice at its nearness, while at the same time we contemplate the starlight that shines on our table and are appalled at the farness of its source. The bread once eaten, we have a most comforting sense of its nearness, and we may even pass our hand over its whereabouts with assuredness that it is there.

But suppose we make our test one of getting to it while it is in course of its electronic incorporation in us, not merely one of passing our hand over it, stepping over it, so to speak, but of getting right down to it. With due allowance for what we really refer to by far and near, and for all the questionable phases of those words, it is certainly a serious problem whether the last star that sends us its light is any further away than the last electron that is keeping us alive. To get to it by steps, not by huge leaps of the imagination, there may be just as many steps to be passed over in the one direction as in the other.

I certainly have no contribution to make upon this interesting question. Anybody can answer it in terms of Euclidean space, but everybody who does must remember that the antinomies of Zeno about motion in that same Euclidean space have never been solved in all the history of thought since his day. And it is not a question of Euclidean space at all any more. It is a question of Action in space-time, in the reality of events.

Our interest here is only to forestall a certain cock-sureness about man and the insides which are assumed to compose him, when we come to considering man really in action in the action of society.

Consider the position of a member of the human race in the cosmos he verbalizes around him in terms of the dictum of space-time, that one second equals 186,000 miles.    We human beings are not speedy or lasting, and we are judging distances and durations, as though real, with tremendous oblique-ness from our slow center.    Our swiftest runner may make 30 feet a second, our swiftest convey-ance 300, our swiftest projectile 3000, but in the meantime we attribute to light waves a billion feet.    If we put the duration of human life on the globe at 100,000 years, and assume that the race has wandered a mile an hour ever since, then in its entire history mankind would have travelled only the distance which light could have covered in an hour and a third.    Light goes 6,600 times that far in a year, and we locate our furthest star clusters at a million of those light years away.

Looking inward into the motions of the materials of our body down to the electrons we have corres-ponding immensities under the squint our language system gives to our experience.    The physicist has a simplified way of stating the facts.    Starting with a unit of one centimeter, about four-tenths of an inch, he expresses distances in powers and inverse powers of that quantity, and the comparison is easy. If the radius of our universe is $10^{22}$ centimeters, he can compare it with the estimate for an electron in a hydrogen atom which has a radius of $10^{-13}$ centimeters. He says that the furthest star is that far "away" from the center but he does not commonly use the same term "away" in talking of the electron, and yet his measured distance as a matter of passage, transition, in space time, is nearly as huge—too huge for us with our slow earthly progresses to give meaning to. The electron, we may say, is billions of light waves "away" from us, and that is about all we can say of the furthest star clusters.

Not in absolute space, Newtonian space, conforming itself complacently to our human foot rule, but in the relativity of space-time, man may just as well forget these distances and measures when he begins to study himself in action. They are forms of his practical statements which he may some day explain to himself in better forms, but which for the present must not be allowed by him to stultify all his other explanations of himself.

Inside and outside, far and near, remote past and distant future, are all right for us as we go about our daily business. Inside and outside are all right for the physiologist studying a cell in its broader manifestations. Far and near are all right for an astronomer comparing two stars in space alone.

But they are nevertheless judgments of men in action in society. They must not be allowed to dominate the study of men in action, but taken rather as they are for part of that action. And we may confidently accept as a delivery to us from the new physics that inside and outside, far and near, are doubtful words, marks of problems, not recognized facts, and possibly not necessary concepts either for physics or for the study of man and society, though that again is for the future to show.

# IX

## The Words "Matter" and "Mind"

Of the words matter and mind a remark or two
may be made.  Beyond that we cannot go here.
To convince any reader who still cleaves firmly to
realities assumed by him to exist behind these two
words, and for whose understanding the words have
not already been broken down and functioned by the
considerations previously set forth, it would be
necessary to present an elaborate argument far beyond the possibilities, purposes or powers of this
essay.  What concerns us is not setting up meanings,
but guarding against the intrusion of hurtful meanings into regions in which they do not belong.

For the physicist the word matter now indicates
little more than one large and vague group of events,
which he contrasts with other groups described as
radiations or electricity, but all of which groups
have recently been approaching a combined treatment under common laws.

As to mind, in the sense of mind-stuff, the psychologists long ago abandoned it. Likewise in all its old categories, such as sensation, feeling, will, it has passed into decay. Through pragmatisms which have accomplished much, into behaviorisms which have accomplished more, the psychologists have come ever more to a study of action, events.

And this action of the living being, this word of the psychologist, becomes more and more friendly to the same word of the physicist. The physicist has passed from an actor in an environment to action, and the psychologist is doing the same. He studies a happening which he cannot study unless he includes its prospective phases with its retrospective. No longer can he give it an instantaneous present. Instead he must give it a present in duration and space which is a full bit of the moving experience.

And again, the space and time of the physicist as they have become better measurable, have become relativities of observation—which is mind.

The practical daily use of matter and mind as words is of course not affected any more than with other terms. It is made susceptible of more intelligent use, so far as our purposes may require it.

# X

## Language and Epistemology

We are men. Man is a word. We know ourselves in terms of language. The language and its words are practical implements. The knowledge of ourselves that we have in terms of this system of practical words is peculiarly weak. We give it body in the age long pattern by exteriorizing the meanings, clotting the references. These clotted references, taken over as foundations for a scientific study of society are not fit for the purpose, not any of them. There has been indeed an ever increasing discard of these dead meanings. Psychology has been at work on them, aided on the one side by the interpretation of experience in physics, and on the other by the provisionally phrased fact accumulations of descriptive sociology.

Certain main threads of the argument concerning language may be assembled. First as to function: words as limits of thought, measurements of thought,

in short, all of thought we have.   Another is the
entirely social nature of language.   Words as appearing only when there is a developed twoness or mul-
tiplicity of posited beings, communications as involving a separation of communicator and communicant.   Again there is the groupal nature of society.
Language as getting all its meanings from the cross-
sectional activities of society, meanings and values
being entirely relativities of such cross sectional or
groupal activities.   Another is the spatial and temporal relativity of this groupal activity: the words
for space and time and velocity and mass already
functioned into the system of knowledge.

Common forms of expression take the word man
and posit a known unit man behind it.   They then
take the word thought and posit a power of the man
to think.   They then take the word language, with
all its comprised words, and posit this as a tool
which man has constructed to help use his power
of thought and to help him make contact conceived
of as external to him with other similar unit men
with their own powers of thought.

Psychology has long ago of course, abandoned such
an approach.   It has man, not posited, but an open
field of study.   It has thought, not as a power,
but a rough description of part of that field.   It
has recently gone far towards identifying language

and thought.   It has not, so far as I know, identified
the language-thought contents with the cross-sectional activities of society.   But then that is not
directly in its field, which is rather the contacts of
process on the physiological side.

The students of anthropology and culture have
examined the historical development of languages in
many forms and groups and families, and they have
made many rich observations connecting these various languages with the actual living processes of the
societies in which they have risen.   Their work
stands out brilliantly on the descriptive side.   There
remains the study of process on the social side,
possible only as we develop in knowledge of the
representative relations established between the
various groupal activities of society, one with another.

We are told that so far back as cultural remains
give us any hints at interpretation of men in their
life together, we find the germinal aspects of religion,
attempts at getting behind and explaining what the
group of men is doing and experiencing.   Fire is
so recent that it has not only its most primitive
aspects of worship or appeasement, but its developed
mythologies.   Mythologies have arisen to explain
the division of men into tribes, and the splitting
up of languages has had many early attempts at

authoritative explanation. But for the fact of speech itself, I do not remember that any mythology has seemed to require an explanation. Language has always been taken for granted. Communication exists among the animals, as a definite means of coordinating action, and we do not know how far back into simple animal organisms we must go before we find it necessary to restrict the definition of our terms, either for communication or for language. An explicit grammar is not a test even for language. An implicit grammar may not be rejected unless we are certain that we catch all the intonations among the communicants and not merely those for our own specialized ear. A sign language might perhaps exist without a voice and ear language accompaniment. We may set our limits arbitrarily for any special study, but not when we are determining all social process.

To say that language and thought must be taken as one activity, is not to announce an intention of building anything on the statement. It is to announce a limiting condition applicable to our present investigations of man in society without committing ourselves as to whether at some other time with an increased knowledge, the limit may be entirely transformed or superseded. It is merely to say that here and now, no matter what of man and society we are studying, we must not attribute characteristics to the one which we do not attribute to the other as a means of explaining one by the other. We may define the aspects as we wish and study them with further limitations as we wish, but we must not do violence to this essential limit in the belief that we are thereby producing an explanation.

The propositions concerning language as social possess just the same kind of values: they are not building blocks, but controls against illusory explanations, at the present stage of our knowledge. Words are created in communication. The subjects of communication are social. The participants in the communications are functioning together in a myriad of ways. The words express this common functioning. The most primitive sense impressions of the world are tied together in this way. The earliest objectifications are built up in language. The very word space was doubtless built up into a meaning in a specialized group, expanded across almost all the members of society, but in different groupal meanings, all of them functioning processes of groups, and it is now being taken apart and reconstructed by a very specialized group, representative in function of other groups with ramifications running wider and wider, until the word will be partially reconstructed or wholly reconstructed among approximately all members of the society.

The world of knowledge is so socially constructed. The world as we objectify it in our finest interpretations as well as in our crudest, is not other than the world of knowledge. Its meanings are all to the social life of man. From the furthest star to the whisk of an electron it has no other type of values than this. Its truth is within knowledge and within language and within society. Its parts have meaning only in a relativity to other parts. There are no tests or standards or judgments applicable to any part except in terms of other parts. Within these limits society must be studied, nor explained outside of them.

Epistemology, the theory of knowledge, subject of much hard struggle in the history of thought, stands today as a superior sort of word analysis. As such it must be taken up into the body of each science by its own tests of coherence under the processes of scientific experiment, prediction and verification.

The epistemology of physics is found in mathematics.

So far from the study of society having an epistemology functioning within itself, it has not even begun to formulate definite terms by means of which all investigators can feel confident that they are specifying approximately the same facts.  Even the term social psychology or psychological sociology used by practically all investigators is so vague that hardly for any two of them has it the same shading of subjectivity or objectivity, yet having some shading of this non-factual distinction in all of them. The simple term instinct taken from psychology, has no set meaning, even admitting its right to transference at all.  The terms of culture are becoming definite so far as they describe tool or custom complexes, but not in distinctions of laws and institutions.  The epistemology of sociology has barely begun as yet to set up the simplest verbal scaffoldings on which the terminological analysis can proceed.

The older epistemology had another aspect besides this one, as it touched the contacts of knowledge with reality.  Such contacts are today not in a plausible field of investigation.  Knowledge, and the world of knowledge, go too far, on the one hand for such an investigation, and on the other hand, not far enough.  The search is like that for perpetual motion, a contradiction in terms.  Such epistemology is an elaborate complicated solemn way of doing what we can do forthwith by letting facts control words, not words facts.

What may develop in this field in the future, after the present task of securing verbal coherence over the unoccupied part of the field has been sufficiently advanced, is of course for the future to show.

# XI

## Consciousness and Man

*Error: Dreams: Ideals:* Procedure by trial and failure, new trial and success, is found in the simplest life forms. It is found in the most complicated processes of men in society.

We may state it in terms of the behavior of a mouse learning its way through a maze to a store of corn. We must then broaden the statement in two directions, first to cover the more complex (or possibly simpler) processes of conscious determination and decision in society; and second to cover the simpler (or possibly more complex) processes of anticipation in what we call lower forms of activity. The physicist working "within" the atom may look aghast at the possibility of an electron in one path having within itself some specification of where its next path must be under given impacts, but still he must look at it.

We have throughout in this field a problem of

durations. Durations, not instantaneousness, is what experience gives us. Duration has both past and future in it. What it does not have is an arbitrary series of instants. The future controls the past as much as the past controls the future: which is to say that each determines the other; which again is to say, with much greater exactness, that neither can be specified and defined, without the specification and definition of the other.

It is because the social fact includes the future, and the future is multiform, which is to say the facts build themselves complexly in durations, that this reference to error is necessary. The procedure of error and its elimination is studied by the psychologists. The durational content, separated by definition for specific study, so far as human activity is concerned, is studied by the sociologists.

On the same grounds dreams and ideals may be referred to and passed to their technical students. Dreams today find their meanings not in some reality shot up behind the words describing them, but in an interpretation of the social and organic life processes. In the hands of the analysts they have been made to yield valuable results.

Ideals, given a social statement, have value in terms of human groups and cross sections of society, like any other social facts. Just because they are projected against a social future, stated in terms of a desired future, does not for an instant deprive them of their direct groupal expressive quality. Their process is again the psychologist's study. And in no matter what mysticism we come finally to the same range of values.

*The Word "Consciousness."* One of our most widely known psychologists, Professor Watson, not only excludes the word "Consciousness" from his work, and with it all such terms as sensation, perception, image, will, attention, but says frankly he does not know what the terms mean and does not believe that anyone else can use them consistently.

It is again only by way of setting guards against error that the following remarks are made.

Consider a definition by which consciousness is made to be a "unique relation which may maintain on occasion between a living organism and its world." So far as the words go, they keep the organism and the world separate, posit a relation, and place this in a series of relations, making it "unique" with respect to all the others of the series. Each of those words has a huge background of possible shadings of meaning. And yet, no matter how we crystallize each of them, the one most probable remark about consciousness is that it is that aspect of experience in which there is a comprehensiveness of organism and world and relationship; that is, in which these words have broken down entirely. And further it is only on the basis of these words that a uniqueness can be asserted.

Of course there are ways of using the terms even in psychology which have a practical value. The psycho-analyst, while confining himself to his practical work, roughly designates the conscious and subconscious fields, as contrasting in function and inhibition. But his usage has no value outside that particular task he is doing, and only the roughest value there.

If this indicates the situation in psychology, where conscious phenomena are a direct subject of study, what is apt to result from the use of the term in the study of society? Examination gives the answer very quickly: classifications which assume everything from the immediate point of view of the student. A typical statement of the series of stages of society or of the types of process in sociologies is first, instinctive combination; next, customary or traditional action; lastly, rational action, with assumed increasing consciousness. And yet the fact that we are today aggressively debating certain particular changes we want in our society, while some small primitive group does not seem to be similarly concerned, does not destroy the possibility, except from our today's point of view, that that small group may be as aggressively debating on matters we are quiescent about, as we are our own matters. We are not open to sense their procedure any more easily than they to sense ours. They show set uniformities to us, and we forget how much we show similar setness to them.

No better are the results when factors like ideas, will, feelings or even instincts are used. The whole development of the study of society in the last fifty years has been a progressive elimination of the terms of individual consciousness and of all other terms of psychology as agents of interpretation of society. Even instincts have been reduced to very small proportions. The point is of course that the social content may not be explained in terms of individual process so long as the individual process itself is defined in terms of social content. Not an explanation, but a repetition of the facts in a different set of terms is given us: which would of course be proper enough if the terms all the way through functioned into one another. But as long as they are held outside of each other in two systems, it is not proper.

We come then to this. A "consciousness" that psychology does not understand may not naïvely be taken as an interpreting agent by a sociologist. Nor may any of its involved terms. Nor may these be expanded into a social consciousness thereby accelerating the vagueness.

The social facts must be studied in their own terms. And these terms must be so defined as not to exclude, and cast out into some other field, say that of the individual man, any of the purposiveness, consciousness, subjectivity, they possess.

That is the limitation, to be transcended when we can coherently transcend it, and not before.

*"What is Man?"* To ask this question in flat terms, considering the many dogmatic answers and their common definite fate under advancing knowledge, is almost to raise a laugh.

And yet, if the "what" is taken to be a scientific what, and if the "Man" is taken to be all the observed activities in all their meanings and values, it is a question which, if very broad, is at any rate entirely legitimate.

The moment we approach it, however, we observe that we have two terms for the same observed phenomena, neither having, so far as I have found in the writings I have studied, any definite description in terms of the other, sufficiently clear to have any large groups of scientific users capable of using them to communicate exactly to one another upon their observations. One is Man. The other is Society.

One can over-personify man, and society becomes a troublesome matter of vague objectivity and vague shadings of reality. One can over-personify society and the individual man becomes an undigested lump in the system. By what right use such a term as "over-personify"! with emphasis on the "over," the excess? Simply because the terms do not function well with our observations of man in society. Something is wrong. The definitions are faulty. The test by facts is confused.

If one can define man and proceed to separate definitions of the individual men, so that the summation of all of them gives an adequate picture of the totality of observations we call society, well and good. Or if one can define this totality of observations satisfactorily without specifying individual men, well and good. Or if one can set apart his social facts here and his individual facts there in good working definitions, well and good. If he cannot do any one of these three things he must break down the words till he gets at the source of the trouble and gets his working statement of facts.

The first of these approaches is the ancient practical point of view, but wherever study of social facts proceeds intensively it has to be at least partially abandoned, and it proceeds to set up an objectified society over and against its man. The second method results in mysticism, worships, wholes that will not be defined, and will not gain adherents, theoretically, beyond small circles. The third approach finds nowhere social facts that are not in men, and nowhere men who are not aspects of society so far as the observations directly under study are concerned. It can define its men in part away from society, but it cannot separate their activities in society from the society that is in them: many trials on each line, but no results of thought or language, which will pass acceptance with exact meanings across groups of special students, so as to enable them to proceed in linked advance: plenty of statements along each line which will be held as satisfactory for some particular social activity and program by some particular group with reference to other particular groups, but none which will stand generalization from all these groupal points of view.

We are forced then to the suspicion that our words, Man and Society are specialized in ways which will not yield to the analysis that is needed.

Our observations, our experiences, then, have brought us to this point. Not only must we refuse to appeal to realities assumed to exist behind these two words. We must throw them both out of our vocabulary in our efforts to describe the social facts, which have been inadequately described in terms of them. We must do this, not by way of settling the question, not by way of having arrived anywhere when we do it, but by way of a requirement, a limitation, on our statements. With what value either or both terms will come back at the end of such a new attempt at statement, is for the results to show, not for us now to anticipate.

What, then, is man? He is all the values that he has ever been, without one whit of deterioration. He is all the values of mind or spirit or soul that he has ever been. He is probably very many more values than these crude words have indicated. Only, he has come to a point where, if he is going to find out what he is, he must abandon for awhile his crude words, abandon even the attempt to read revised meanings into them, he must let them go entirely for the present. He must even forget to bother about what he is, directly or indirectly, and learn to describe and handle these activities of living and changing from a past into a future, which have refused to yield a solid meaning under the terms he has used.

*Man as the Universe.* A bit of speculation may deserve consideration. Again, not as specified knowledge, but as provisional limitation. A limitation, two ways.

It is old enough—the substance of many philosophies—and new enough—the contribution of the latest physics.

Space and time and energy have come into knowledge, as variables within it. Knowledge has come into language, as having no other home. And language comes to be the most certainly social fact, at once individual thought and social statement.

Lacking terms for the man-society field, call it for the moment X. The universe is in X and X is in the universe. The quality of "in-ness" cancels out. The universe and the man-society field are on the face of it something given together. We have no right to call them the same. That would mean nothing, except as related to some group purpose or activity or man-society. We are nevertheless under compulsion, as a limitation to our examination, not to posit anything that directly or indirectly purports to explain one by the other. Not until we have facts and terms working so we can handle them, at any rate.

In knowledge, physics, the advance is well under way towards expressing the full world facts in terms of electrons or what it may prove to be. In knowledge, man-society, the process is under way of expressing the electrons in terms of social activity. Space-time, durations, anticipations, form the unifying thread.

Not in Man, the old individual of definition, rests this knowledge-universe.  It rests in this X, this man-society field of examination.

* * * * *

Lacking language, words, definitions, terms which relate themselves definitely together, so that they carry exact meanings to at least enough people to make up an audience, even to a most limited investigating group, I have been compelled to build up this argument by foreshadowing, by using overlapping lines of word structure, striving only, at some point in the development, to bring out each such line to a definite statement, interpreting its prior use and justifying it, and consolidating the way to the next step.

This preliminary development should now be finished, and it should be possible, even without technical terms which can only come into use by the cooperation and agreement of many workers, to make a comparatively exact statement of the propositions in regard to the study of man-society, as an introduction to which this preliminary survey has been necessary.

# PART III

# OUR KNOWLEDGE OF SOCIETY

## Analysis

# XII

## Man-Society

§ 1. *The Opposition of Individual to Society in Current Discussion.* The opposition of individual to society is one of wide discussion. It appears in many sociologies, some of which are so fascinated by it that they seem to make the modes of personality their central thought. It appears in studies of ethics, in debates on legislation, and in a thousand and one discussions of modern life.

That there is a real meaning underlying this opposition is certain. But it is equally certain that in these varied discussions the meaning is not always the same, and indeed not always even of the same type. This is because in every one of these discussions there is a background of meaning assumed or at most only partially expressed. This background meaning, unseen and unstated, controls and governs the discussion, and by that token provides the limitations to its validity. We shall find later that this background meaning rests always in some particular activity or set of activities of some section of the population, and can be defined only in terms of these activities.

§ 2. *The Problem of Individual and Society in Science.* Suppose now that we wish to pass beyond such special discussions, and bring out the relations of the individual to society on a basis which we can use scientifically. Let scientifically mean to us nothing more and nothing less than such an arrangement of defined terms as can be used with reasonable exactness in all studies by agreement of all or almost all of the workers in the field.

No one today tries to describe the individual as he finds him, except in social terms, no matter how he may theoretically define him. Some investigators define society, usually in the terms of the social mind, as apart from or exterior to all individuals. But even these, unless they avoid entirely the question of the location of this super-individual society, must locate it in individual men and nowhere else.

We face then this situation that society seems to consist of the individuals, and the summation of the individuals seems to be society. Such being the case a discussion of the relation of the individual as such to society as such can have no exact meaning. We must change our statement to that of the relation of the individual to other individuals. And again not to all other individuals, but to a certain part of them, whether past or future, or scattered in the space of the present. And still again, if we wish to be exact, the question comes whether we can examine the relation of a complete individual to other complete individuals, or only certain aspects of one individual to certain aspects of other individuals.

I believe the whole series of questions so put to be impossible of solution in scientific generalization. The best we can do by their aid is to indicate society on the one hand, and the individual on the other, as rough descriptive terms: that is, as the location of problems, not as elements in the analysis of problems.

I put no stress on the argument of this section. I deem it correct, but do not regard it as necessarily carrying weight with others. The real question is not as to the exactness of such argument but as to the relative value of different forms of statement. The question is: Can we do better? That is what we have to see.

§ 3. *The Term Man-Society*. In the preceding chapter I have used the term Man-Society to cover the field of investigation, omitting all advance determination as to either individual man or society; omitting with these all advance determinations of the characteristics of the individual man, that is, all psychological factors accepted with the definition suitable to psychology on the one side; and on the other all advance determinations of society, whether in its description of subject or actor or as environment to the individual. We have before us a great range of facts called social and found in the living procedures of individual men, and these it is our task to face and examine as directly as we may to see what they yield us as we find them together and unseparated by antecedent definition.

§ 4. *Definitions.* We must use a few terms with precise meanings. We shall choose them for immediate use with the smallest practicable modification from common vague or double meanings. These terms are:

MAN-SOCIETY. Let it designate the general field of investigation, the locus of the facts we are to examine, without committing us in advance to theories about those facts, drawn from other experience or other study.

ACTIVITY. Any happening or event or procedure in man-society. The term carries with it extension, duration and energy as viewed in Euclidean space. It does not, however, restrict us to experience that has been commonly reported in Euclidean terms—that is, it does not exclude the mental in man.

CROSS-SECTIONAL ACTIVITY. Any activity in its characteristic as appearing across a group of men. It is definable only in terms of a number of men, but not in terms of any or all of those men, qua individuals.

REPRESENTATIVE ACTIVITY. The characteristic of any cross-sectional activity by which it can be defined only in terms of other cross-sectional activities, involving all their anticipatory features, and involving all and more than is meant when the vaguer term purposiveness is used with reference to them.

SOCIAL FACT. Any definable situation in man-society. If given an abstract statement, as for example statistical, it has meaning only as referred to cross-sectional activity.

§ 5. *The Usage of Other Words.* In the above definitions the word group has substantially the meaning of cross-sectional. It would have been here used by preference for cross-sectional, had it not such concrete reference to a total of individual men, that it tends to divert attention from the common activity by which alone the group is characterized. It has been much used in recent sociology though without sufficient definiteness of meaning, and it will very possibly prove to be the term which sociology will adopt for the type of fact under consideration.

The word purposiveness as used is taken to cover not only the explicit or conscious purposings, but the larger and little explored purposive processes in what the psycho-analyst calls the sub-conscious and which are themselves a direct subject of study in the social field.   In the line of investigation here followed out the purposive aspects appear as specializations of still wider process.

The words man and society as used occasionally, either refer to usages by other investigators, or must be taken as casual references without implication beyond what is permitted in the definition of man-society.

# XIII

## The Social Fact

§ 6. *Concrete Determinations of the Social Fact.* Speculations are common as to what facts concretely taken may be regarded as social and what not social. Often these speculations present themselver in the guise of exact delimitation. They may lay off a pre-social field of human activity in the evolutionary series. Or they may lay off an extra-social individual field in present experience.

It is evident that every such concrete determination has as its controlling background a mass of opinion, mostly inchoate. Its technical importance depends on what that inchoate mass would show if analyzed.

I do not pretend to know what determinations of this type, if any may ultimately be made. I am confident that none of them have any special value at the present time. If made for pedagogical purposes, they must be subject to continuous alteration as our knowledge of social procedure increases. They are at best descriptive and not helpful as tools of investigation, however pleasing otherwise.

§ 7. *The Social Fact as Cross-Sectional Activity.* The social fact will be for us, as has been said, any definable situation in man-society, involving for its full definition statement in terms of activity, which is always cross-sectional. Should any one contend at the present time that there are facts of man-society that are not cross-sectional activity, the burden of proof is on him, and he must draw his arguments, not out of a fund of knowledge, but out of a fund of ignorance; ignorance of course being not a negative condition, but a great positiveness in defective statement. I am not asserting here that there are no such facts, but only as a guide to work, that the tendency is towards including them all in a statement of cross-sectional activity.

§ 8. *Value of the Word Activity.* The word activity has no magic value in connection with social facts. Its function is that of a common denominator. In a similar way the word behavior has served as a common denominator in the newer psychology. The service the word renders us can appear only in its practical use. We may locate part of our social facts in a space world and part in a non-space world, mind or psyche. We may find that this is not enough and that we must have a locus for social facts in a non-spatial social mind or social soul. Many forms of both these types of statement are current. Or we may discard both types as scaffoldings that have been useful enough in their day and are now no longer needed. Then we shall be looking at the social facts direct, and if we call them activity, that is simply the word that indicates what we are doing.

§ 9. *A Social Fact-Complex, the Volstead Law.* We handle our social facts by a process, sometimes crude, sometimes careful, of examining, analyzing, defining and redefining. As we shall see later this entire process itself rests in the group participations we ourselves share while doing this work.

Let us take a social fact or fact-complex, any one. Take the Volstead Law, federal prohibition of alcoholic drinks. What do we have? A set of words, an enacting clause, many printed copies.

When we have said that, have we said anything? Hardly, unless we carry with those words a great unexpressed background of reference. Let us set down some of those background references, not by way of being complete or by way of discussing the Volstead Law, but merely for illustration of the material.

A vote of Congress. The signature of the Presi-

dent.  Many days of debate in Congress.  Many
weeks of committee hearings.  Very, very many
man-years of lobbying for and against.

A constitutional amendment.  All of its attendant
efforts.  Its submission to the states.

State and community law and ordinance experiences, local option and prohibition.

A generation or two of writing, speaking, organization, public meetings, addresses, editorials.  Temperance societies, prohibition societies, political parties and platform planks.  Brewers', distillers', and
retailers' organizations.  Chemists' investigations.

Circles of discussion widening out into principles
of government and rights of man.

A changed industrial system, division of labor,
machinery, motors.

A changing food complex.

A cross-section of the courts, judges, attorneys,
marshals.

A welter of private attorneys, legal points, technicalities, relations to other laws and to the constitution, and the supreme court at last.

A new staff of investigators in the treasury depart-
ment.

A new mass of law-breakers, differently law-
breaking.

Some new reaches and magnitudes of corruption.

A change in expenditures and in lives, in durations and experiences of men's lives. Disease changes, jail changes.

§ 10. *Its Full Statement in Terms of Activity.* In all this, and in all the many aspects here unmentioned, there is activity, and nothing that may not be characterized as activity, however variously that activity may be analyzed. There is nothing that is not human, there is nothing that is not social, down to the last grain grown for spirits, down to the last effect on human tissue. Any or all of it may for some special purpose be viewed otherwise, but no such other viewing may exclude the human and social viewing.

§ 11. *Special Meanings for the Term "Volstead Law."* Let us see next in a few illustrations, how this Volstead law fact-complex is described or defined from different points of view in society.

The publisher will see in the law the printed words, but even he must run his statement back into terms of paper makers and type-setters and printers and binders and business managers.

A newspaper man may see live news, all in terms of many activities of many people.

Courts and lawyers will see prescriptions of action established under technical status of title and enacting clause, records of congress and coherence with constitution, and perhaps indeed many active influences outside of these.

Law enforcement officials will see a manner of action to be followed.

Law breakers will see a manner of action to be avoided by substituting other action.

Citizens will see a changing action which they call perhaps, a great step in human progress, or perhaps an infringement on the rights of man.

But for all of these the statement when pushed down to completeness is in terms of men's ways of doing things, not dead, but parts of their vital lives, with meanings all in terms of other ways of doing, equally parts of their social living.  Activities are touching, combining, opposing, mastering, representing, interpreting one another.  The very words of discussion are activities of similar values.

And in every one of these statements of the law from such various quarters the statement makes itself in terms of the very activities the different elements of the population are themselves participating in.  They are practical expressions right out of social activity, and they may or may not be capable of being taken up into that different type of statement which can be generalized and termed scientific. There is a concealed rhetorical subject in every one of the above statements and in all similar statements: it is some particular group activity in which the man who makes the statement is a participant.

§ 12. *Technical Meaning in Durations, Extensions and Energies.* Pass now from these practical statements to consider the requirements of a scientific statement; one, that is, that will function with all the other statements and provide a basis for advancing understanding.

First, the query whether we have above stated one fact or more than one fact, or less than one fact. That is purely a practical question to be answered in accordance with the needs of any particular investigation. Any particular determination or limitation of the facts for study will be in terms of durations, extensions and energies that can be handled in the existing state of our knowledge in the particular field.

We may run a temperance-prohibition study back into early civilizations or out across the surface of the globe. When we take it in energies however, we will map out special fields. For the United States we may go back perhaps fifty years. We will perhaps identify it with present industrial organizations. We will then observe activity connections of a different type, in Maine, Kansas and the South. We may establish boundaries conforming with certain phases of the trading system as differentiated from the producing organization. Perhaps on one or another line we can combine in one field all of western Europe with the United States, requiring for that an extension of durations possibly into the near future. We may or may not find a possibility of extension across the Russian field, and still more remotely across the Mohammedan field. We will watch the contacts with other activities across government controls and through opinion and discussion.

With durations, extensions and energies we will get specifications that will enable us to make reasonably exact reports of what is going on here or there, and reasonably valuable comparisons of differences in the procedure in different extensions or durations and activity complexes.

§ 13. *Is the Law Beyond These Activities?*  Assuming all this, there is another phase of the question: Have we stated more or less than a fact?  Have we left out something that is social or something that is individual?  Have we added anything perhaps to the assumed individual, that we have no right to add?

The fact-complex that we ran over presents itself to us with the special label or tag, a "law."  Studies of law during the last century, centering on the problem of how the law stood in its control over the individual culminated in great structural philosophies, which gave the law a mystic sphere above the individuals of society. Combined with similar studies in other branches of political science these philosophies centered their attention on sovereignty, which gave the sanctions for the law, and existed in super-social quality, ideal, absolute, reality, of a nature that required great ingenuity to discuss.

Do we lose anything of this if we confine ourselves to a full statement of the complex of activities in man-society? Certainly not if the tendency of studies in political science the last fifteen or twenty years is any guide. Such studies have been working away from the absolute sovereignty and the mystic law. They have been locating the energies here and there and everywhere, describing and summing them. The work is not complete but the tendency is towards the position here taken. The theories of a social mind, superior and external to the individuals, are bound to head in the same direction. The more the analysis of activities proceeds the less excuse is there for projecting the law out of human nature upon some idealistic sky, where it has a reality and a power of its own and in its own definition.

§ 14. *Is Something of the "Individual" Left Out of its Statement?* The individual, is he left out?

Against the mystic sovereignty and law he had his place in opposition. But as all the activities that he carries are brought into the interpretation, his place in opposition fades out, tends to disappear. The activities that make the law are nowhere else than in the individuals, all of them. All that remains is the question whether there are some activities in the individual that do not take the social description and definition. And that again together with the question of their practical importance, if there are any, is a question which is not for answer today. The tendency, the working guide of study, is towards their inclusion. Of this more will be said later.

§ 15. *The Answer in Terms of Working Probabilities.* The question as to whether a statement in terms of activities in man-society mutilates the facts, or presents them too bare, too thin, must be answered in terms of working rules, of probabilities in study.

If statements in terms of factors of individual psychology have shown a steady tendency to reconstruction in such way as to eliminate most of these terms and leave the rest without terminological agreement among the workers who use them; if the statements in social terms are expanding and giving promise of terminological agreement; and if the psychological terms tend to show themselves, not so much as errors, but rather as crude approximations to the values of the social statements, then not merely is the probability in favor of the social statement, but it becomes scientific requirement that these statements should be carried out to develop their full value. And not until it becomes apparent, if it ever does, that a sacrifice is involved by way of losing the full purposiveness of social procedure, will the tendency be checked or a turn made in the other direction.

XIV

## Cross-Sectional Activity

§ 16. *Typical Cross-Sectional Activities of the Volstead Law.* Continuing the use of the Volstead Law for illustrative purposes, let us pick out of the great mass of activity some typical specifications, cross-sectional to society, each carried in the lives of a group of the men in the society.

First perhaps a pleasure custom, the use in the United States, or in more detail, in this or that section of the states, of a certain particular small number of the many kinds of alcoholic drinks which history reports here or there, at one time or another, to have been used. These drinks we find taken, with a definite range of alcoholic percentage, under definite form of manufacture and distribution, and above all in definite social situations, with their proper conventions as to times, places and methods, varying with different sections of the populations.

Or it may be that in partial replacement of the definition as a pleasure custom we shall find it necessary to define some of this drinking activity as a relaxation of tension, a release-function from the strains of other intersecting socially defined activities.

Again it may appear as a food process, varying in character and definition with different types of diet.

Another statement will be in terms of domestic activities, expenditures, comforts, health, child rearing, violence; or in terms of petty crimes, jails, wastes, politics.

Again we have it in terms of industrial organization, centralized steam plants, transportation efficiency, scattered small gasoline power plants, distributed electricity, mass production.

And then, of course, there are the statements of it as a business process, production of raw materials, manufacture and trade.

§ 17. *Every Such Cross-Sectional Activity May be Defined Only in Terms of Other Cross-Sectional Activities.* Start with certain statistics, say the number of gallons of liquor produced, imported, consumed per capita, and the figures may truly be written down barely as facts. But whoever writes them down, and calls them facts no matter who he is— unless perhaps the statistician, for whom the assembling of the figures is a direct first-hand activity

—presents with them, whether explicitly or implicity, some one or more of the many cross-sectional activities, of which a few examples have been given above. And somewhere in this background is his real definition of the facts he is presenting.

True enough it is very common to generalize the whole situation into a drink habit which may be presented as social, and over against which is set some trait of human nature which is posited in offset as individual. But the "drink habit" and the "human nature" are as bare and meaningless as the statistics, until they are worked out and specified in these defined activities. And the more completely this specification is carried out, the less importance the emphasis on the habit and the human nature retains.

When we have the whole situation spread out before us in as many specifications as we can reach, we have it all as activity in man-society. And in addition to this we have all these activities defined in terms of other activities in man-society. We can define no one of them except in terms of others. And the more thoroughly we succeed in this process of definition the less we have of any factors outside of it to carry or give body to our interpretations.

§ 18.　*Contrast with "Outside" Causes and Effects.* I freely admit an apparent repulsiveness in this statement that the definition of each social activity must be in terms of other social activities. The antipathy hooks up, perhaps, with our long linguistic habit of explaining things by things "outside" of them. Nevertheless, I am forced to the attitude here taken by practical experience in dealing with social facts, and the antipathy has got to yield.

The crude cause and effect statement of the type of the billiard player, the cue and the billiard ball (the player "aims" and the cue "pushes" the ball), however satisfactory it is in its place, is too thin and poor for interpretative use in the study of man-society. We may get certain approximations by saying in one place that the drinking custom produces the drinking trade, or in another that the drink trade forces the drinking custom. For this use or that we can emphasize a cause side and an effect side to explain an increment here or an increment there but for our wide general uses, we must take these and many other activities together, and let the understanding, the very definition of each be in terms of others. Get these cross-sectional activities as carefully analyzed and differentiated as possible, stated in terms of one another and we really begin to comprehend what is going on.

§ 19. *Illustration from Planes in a Euclidean Solid.* One may draw a comparison of these activities in man-society with planes in a Euclidean solid. The planes intersect along lines, the lines at points. In three dimensions although we may say there is an infinite number of planes, the scheme is very simple. But, as has been said in Euclidean space it would take ten dimensions to compute for Einstein what with Riemann's geometry could be computed in four: and it has been suggested that mental phenomena may ultimately require statement in some unknown number and variety of dimensions beyond those of space and time.

We can conceive of these cross-sectional activities of man-society as qualitatively dimensional, and intersecting in the individuals of the society. The individual will answer to his name and respond to his characterization as the locus of this intersection, under certain rough descriptive terms of temperament, mental and moral qualities, habits, conduct, social position and so on. If the whole process of man-society can ultimately be described in terms of the cross-sectional planes, that will bring no hurt to the individual as an intersection of many planes, but instead give him in the end, if needed, much fuller and better characterization.

It is to be remembered, of course, that what we have in society is not abstracted surfaces, but activities, with duration, extension and energy aspects.

Observation of them gives them to us in this way.

The illustration in terms of planes is thin and poor, but for all that in a slight degree helpful. Counting human heads, we have different groups of individuals in each plane, each group taken not as so many men as individual wholes with a space line around them, but as a group activity formed of this one aspect of the lives of the men counted in it, that aspect an activity, the connections and constructions of which are to be determined through hard and careful search, free from extraneous prior determinations by non-functioning terms: the statement of that aspect as activity having precedence over the statement in terms of individual men.

§ 20. *Further Phases to be Examined.* The government and discussion and opinion phases of social process are all cross-sectional activities, like those we have been considering, having their values and meanings and definitions in terms of other activities. We shall proceed to examine them from this point of view in the next two chapters, and then pass to further consideration of the individual men as they must be taken account of by us in the scientific study, that is the general study, of man-society.

# XV

## Representative Activity: Governmental

§ 21. *Specialized Representative Activities.* While all cross-sectional activities in man-society require statement in terms of other cross-sectional activities, there are certain types of this relationship, which can be set apart for special consideration, under the term representative. The ones we shall proceed to examine we shall call governmental and opinionative. First the way other activities, not described as governmental or opinionative in this specific meaning of the terms, are represented in the processes of government, whether the outcome of the process is their furtherance or hindrance. And second the way they are represented in the activities of discussion and opinion. We have, that is, specialized activities in man-society which we call governmental or opinionative, and the particular characterization of them in respect to other activities we call representative.

Take again illustration from the Volstead law
facts. There are the lobbyings, committee hearings, discussions and votings of Congress leading
to the passage of the constitutional amendment,
the submission of that amendment to the states and
its ratification by them, the lobbyings, committee
hearings, discussion and votings of Congress leading
to the enactment of the law, the presidential signature, the new structure in the treasury and attorney
general's departments, the rules and regulations
issued, the work of the courts and marshals, the
attorneys on the side of the government, and of
individuals, the fining and jailing processes.   In all
of these we have activities which have their fullest
meaning and best definitions in terms of many other
activities not specifically described as governmental.

One might pick out, perhaps, the presidential
signature, as an individual act in contrast, say, to
the votes in Congress, which are clearly not even
votes except in the system of action to which they
belong.   But even the use of the presidential pen
at a given moment to sign the law is only individual
when described as seen through a very special peep
hole.   The fact that it is found as one man's act
at a special moment and point in space is not unique,
for no other part of the process is found in any different way: everything always is in some man at

some time and place.　The act itself has no meaning or value except in terms of the meanings and values of the rest of the act.　And again the presidential signature is official, presidential, in no way personal, and as such is activity within the wider system.

§ 22.　*Representative Government:　Narrower and Wider Meanings.*　The term representative has had well defined technical uses, in several sciences, but it is the use of it in political science and in ordinary descriptions of government from which the present extension of meaning derives.　A representative government is technically one in which decisions are made by representatives chosen, usually by localities, for limited terms to act individually for their constituents and in combination for the nation. In this sense it stands in contrast with monarchies, aristocracies, oligarchies, hierarchies and other types.

It has become evident, however, to the newer political science that a real representative process in a wider sense exists in all types of government. A monarchy, on a hereditary basis, has this representative characteristic, even though it stretches across a number of generations, even though the technique of its foundation and termination is not that of the ballot, even though its abuses are of a different type, sometimes, than those of a republic, even though its description of itself may be in terms of divine right.

The further extension of the term here consists in making the statement not in terms of individuals as such, but in terms of the activities which they bear and in which they participate.

§ 23. *Power and Government.* Our illustration is of government, but it must be remembered that government is not unique, but a specialized form of all the power phases of man-society. The representative aspect of activity exists in all power procedures. All the activities have their energies capable of determination, and what we recognize as force and power is only a specialization of energy. The power we may find in a domestic field or an economic field or a religious field or any other field. We are not here forming a sociology, and the illustration will be confined to government.

§ 24. *Current Forms of Argument About the Position of "the Representative."* Much ingenuity has been used in analyzing and discussing the relation which a representative, such as we have in our United States Congress, bears to his constituents, and it may be referred to here as illustrating the final barrenness of all similar arguments bearing on the relation of individual to individual in social life. On one side it is argued that the representative should find the purpose of his constituents, or perhaps of that part of them who voted for him, and further it. On the other side it is argued that the representative is a theoretical man, an individual, a personality, detached, free, and put in his place to use his own mind as best he can. A variant, among many variants, makes the representative the bound agent of the formally expressed program of the political party to which he adheres. Another says that the will of the nation should control him.

Such arguments have no more value than the old discussion of free will and determinism which have proved in the very process of discussion to be so meaningless that one rarely hears of them seriously any more, however much this or that individual may retain his personal preference, his hobby, on the subject. With every such theory, we shall find that it is itself part of the opinionative expression of cross-sectional activities in which the advocate of the theory participates.

§ 25.   *Types of Representative Government in Political Science*. Representative government presents itself to start with as an electoral system. Within a large district, defined by geographical boundaries, a country, let us say, to avoid the implications of state, nation or government, are set up smaller districts, and these are subdivided again into still smaller, perhaps several times running, till we reach neighborhood sub-divisions. The American Congress uses the states for senators and congressmen at large and the congressional districts for the remaining congressmen. As contrasted with this territorial representation, a different type of electoral system, based on a small number of classes was common in the middle ages, as houses of nobles, clerics and commons: or in the trades organizations of free cities. A type in some respects akin to this latter appears in the Russian soviets, which give occupational representation, in certain combinations with territorial divisions.

Confining ourselves for a very brief sketch to the American congressional system, and stating it in the most schematic way, merely as illustration, we find it presenting itself to start with, as a list of citizens cut into divisions territorially, each division to pick its best member, and all of these members to get together as individual men in their quality of best men, and to use their exceptional personal equipment to decide on the problems in which all are interested; under an arrangement of checks and balances.

Now what the system said about itself was never what it was, and that fact rapidly came to light in very tangible forms.

First of all the parties, these presenting themselves as agencies of opinion, but themselves not being what they said they were even at the start.

Later on the highly organized self-perpetuating parties, culminating apparently in their machines, but these machines again in time revealing tangibly powerful organized masteries behind them.

§ 26. *Types of Representative Process.* Starting thus with a mere statement of electoral technique, we find we cannot state it at all in a way that has any valuable social meaning without arriving at a very complicated set of cross-sectional social representations. Several types of these representations at once appear.

The parties as they present themselves are cross-sectional. Their programs too are cross-sectional, and not always identical in section with the parties as considered separately from their programs; for the parties in this aspect almost at once show a certain inertia or fixation in the party name, a retarding of motion as between party and opinion allegiance, definable, in part at least, in complexes of opinion statement.

Pursue the analysis and we find what have been called interest groups of the population, activities definable, without too much stress on the word as interests, within the society.

As the party takes on a longer durational form and tighter organization, we find a triple representation, the addition being the representation by the party leadership of the interest group of its workers.

Outside the party structure the stronger interest groups take on their own political organization, the leaders representing the members and establishing interest representations to and fro with the party structure, visible, and invisible.

The representatives in Congress, their elections and their actions, are all presented to us in this complicated net work of representation of activity.

§ 27. *Possible Measurement of Forces Involved.* This rough sketch, this mere series of indications of fact, is shown in a developing differentiation. But it must not be assumed for a moment that there is typical material at the end of the series not present at the beginning. At the end of the series the different factors stand out much more plainly to observation, but a thorough enough analysis of the early conditions would also show the full complex present.

And by the same token, how much is present that we do not yet see clearly is a matter not of assumption or guess work, but of long and difficult study.

A law is passed. We do not really understand this law until we have got the full study of representative connections made. The effects are as much in what is not done on the surface as in what is done. Words and doctrines, those used in the procedure and those we use about it, "interests" those that are on the surface in the procedure and those we trace in their hiding places, must all be established in their social values before we have knowledge.

There is a possibility of measurement in this process, measurement in the sense that forces and values can be established in degrees that get common acceptance through a full group of workers who adopt a common plane of inspection. And even where there is not yet such acceptance there can be an understanding of the nature of the disagreement, and a trend towards its resolution.

§ 28. *Representativeness in Absolute Monarchies.* All of this is true also with the most absolute monarchies. They are called absolute only in describing the external forms of the process. They are not absolute in any sense that excludes full representativeness when we get down to their working process. Absolute monarchies, limited monarchies, aristocracies, theocracies, obligarchies, parliamentary governments, republics, and for that matter clans and tribes and hordes, have all cross-sectional and representative structure. The master's fist in the slave's face, and the slave's reaction to the master, even to his last cringing, are all in this process.

§ 29. *Application to "State," "Nation," "Sovereignty."* What can we say of the whole country in its governmental aspect? The mysterious state, with its personalizing of society, the mysterious nation, with its personalizing of extra-social individual human characteristics, the mysterious sovereignty with its awful authority, disappear. They are not with us any longer, even as technical words when the full representational analysis of activities has been made. They are merely descriptive references. The meaning those words then have will be in terms of the process that has been analyzed.

We may perhaps say that the term state indicates a great complex of closely coinciding activities, which hold together, and get enough representative process for stability. The state is fundamental not as a mystic being but only in the sense of this stability, this durational extent, this relative permanence. The term sovereignty seems to indicate the combined pressure of the specialized activities of government, outward toward other states, and inward on its own separate activities. The term nation seems to indicate similar phenomena with tendencies if there has been some territorial wrenching apart to reincorporation. These but as intimations of what may some day appear to be appropriate statements. The term government, however, is more definite, for it can even now be traced directly into and stated in terms of the more actively changing or the more strongly consolidated cross-sectional interest groups.

Does some communist strive to destroy the "State," or some anti-communist allege that the communist is trying to destroy it. On either side it can only be in terms of some special definition of the state identifying the state with certain of the cross-sectional activities of man-society. Is such an issue drawn with power on both sides imperilling the process of the vaster complexes of activity? What other avoidance of violence, slow and repressive, or sudden and many directioned, except in advancing exactness of statement of interest meanings. Exactness, truth, is of course not the intention of any of the statements as we find them as activities. Fists and guns, votes and words are merely different social techniques in a common process. But the words may submit themselves to finer discriminations and adjustments, and doubtless will when enough of our activities press hard enough upon them to force them into better functioning shapes.

# XVI

## Representative Activity: Opinionative

§ 30. *Opinion as Activity.* The next fact-group to be examined in its characteristic of representative activity, includes the platform and principle phases of politics, political theory, public opinion, similar opinion phases of all other activity in man-society, all systems of ideas and words and language.

In our Volstead law illustration we go back to early temperance campaigns, and organizations, beginning far-off in the pleadings of the "cranks," organizing in early temperance societies, developing into theories and projects of regulation of the liquor traffic, programs and organization for local option and prohibition, moral exhortations connecting the whole process with absolute or divine law, theories of the rights of man and personal liberty, theories of the proper function of law and government, theories of the constitution, of technicalities of the constitution and laws and legal procedure, arguments, exhortations and appeals of endless variety.

This all presents itself in words, spoken and printed, and words are activities of man-society, cutting across the other activities and representing them in a myriad ways. In a sense, possibly regarded as merely analogy, every one will admit that these opinions and theories are activities and that they are representative in their meanings, purposes, references. But that is not enough. The question here is not even whether this is more than an analogy, and indeed a true description, but beyond that whether it is a full description; whether when the representative nature of these phenomena as themselves activities has been brought out we will have a full statement of them, with nothing more beyond that is overlooked or neglected. That "nothing-more-beyond" of course must be taken within the limits of present scientific investigation, and with no limitation upon any science that we may later attain to, and with no restriction on any possibility of ultimate truth to which we may aspire.

§ 31. *Again the Individual and the Absolute Meaning.* Again we face the question as to whether such description leaves out the actual individual on the one side and the absolute truth on the other. All the idea systems present themselves with a claim to be the thoughts of individuals. And all the words they use, under the prevailing idolatry of language, present themselves with claim to carry absolute determinations of truth and reality. Their pretenses need not influence us. They are activities and every bit of their meaning is in terms of other activities. They refuse to tell the story of what those other activities are. They tell only what they choose. It is part of their absolutism that they hide their heads ostrich-like in the sands. Their system is a system of voices arising from the sands of absolutism, and they ignore or deny the exposed rumps of fact which they refuse to recognize or know. It is the problem of the student of society to reveal the rumps of the system and to get the sand smothered voices interpreted in terms of other and wider man-society relativities.

§ 32. *Public Opinion.* Let us examine first public opinion, because it is comparatively fluid, and because its examination is least hampered by the set terminologies of explanation. Recent volumes by brilliant writers have given us most interesting discussions of public opinions in many countries and under many conditions. Their lack is in a clear-cut vision of just what kind of phenomena is studied, just what its reference to other phenomena involved. They are compelled to use some form of individual psychology as a basis. Then they have the questions: Is public opinion a sum of individual opinions or an abstract statement of them? Is it a characteristic of many individual opinions, or is it a psychic phenomenon, not individual? If this latter where is its locus with respect to the individual? These questions may not be explicitly raised: in appearance they may be avoided: but willy-nilly they are structural to every study, and influence its development. The individualistic interpretation was never more than a dictum of the specialist, and Einstein has now placed on it its limitations. The behavior interpretation requires the actor-environment bifurcation, perfectly good in its field but not giving expression to the socially observed fact.

We have writing and printing activities definable on their mechanical and business sides. We have the lecture platform and the stump speech. We have the street corner argument and the home discussion and the casual remark between spadefuls. We have the propaganda, the information and misinformation. The public opinion is all about some activity or activities of man-society. It concerns explicitly or tacitly some program of different activity in man-society. Its information and misinformation are all provided strictly on the basis of other activities. It itself is such activity.

Every one of us as a bearer of public opinion or participant in it is also a participant in a great

number of other activities, and his garnering, select-
ing and expression goes on in this nest of activities.
Every contributor to public opinion proceeds in
just such a net. What he says, what he knows of
what he is doing is a detail. What he is doing is
our fact.

Try to determine exactly what public opinion is,
at any particular moment of some pending issue.
It must be examined in its "for" and "against,"
and the many variations of these: in its locations
and quantities and durations and energies. The
minute one does this it stands out in terms of other
activities of the participants, and nothing else. At
any stage or for any phase, we may count heads,
or try to count them, estimate intensity and spread
and development and change. If the pending issue is
war, we have it not merely in terms of adventure, of
sons and soldiers, of killings and disease, of taxes
and wastes and profiteerings, but of a myriad activities, sectioning themselves variously in localities,
occupations and groups down to the individuals as
last locus, but always whether in the nation or in
one region or one class of it or in the individual
showing themselves as expressions of man-society
activities.

The representativeness is no other, when we strip
off the dead terms of psychology, the dead opposi-

tion of actor and environment, than the representativeness of other activities: of "getting-a-living"
and industrial organization; of peaceable living and
police service; of an urgent corporation and a new
law; of a hampered consumption and another law.
The opinion activities are from one point of view
technique to other activities which are seen developing themselves through them; from another they
are technically related to each other and can be so
studied. But in such ways alone can their meanings and values be brought out.

§ 33. *The More Fixed Opinion Systems.* All that
is true of public opinion in its various stages of
fluidity is true of the more set opinion, theories and
doctrines, through to the final stage of living and
dying faith.

Take any tough argument of political science, say
one as to whether our present development is towards too much law, too many statutes. From the
most casual opinion up to the most carefully elaborated argument there is nothing presented to us
which has meaning except in terms of specific cross-
sectional activities of man-society. The opinion and
arguments do not ever state to us what they represent in full. They tell part and they universalize
their reference. But analyze them and they always
come down to direct meaning and reference in terms

of activity.  There alone are their values to be
found.  One theory may say: "We have too many
laws, we are breaking down as a nation under a
mass of laws."  Yes, but there are some laws the
theorist wants to keep, which others want to reject,
and some which he wants to reject which others
want to keep.

Does that not tell the whole story?  Refer to the
social whole or refer to human nature in the individual.  It may sound satisfying as you write the words.
But have you any further meaning of value?  It
is again the social whole from your present point of
view, and human nature from your present point
of view.  It is again the reflection and expression of
cross-sectional activities which the last bit of argument embodies.

§ 34.  *Ideals. Utopias.*  Ideals? Utopias? They
are the same.  They choose their durations and
locations in time, but they also choose their human
nature and their social wholes out of the cross-sectional contacts of short experienced durations.  Their
whole meanings are founded in experiences, which
are participations in activity.

A world of altruists cast up on our Ideal Sky?  A
world of pacifists now and forever rejecting war?
Our active pacifists are brave people today.  As
social protagonists representing certain definite activ-

ity interests of society, they are pugnacious. They have to be if they are to be representative under their conditions today.

But make a society out of none but pacifists selected from present society. Multiply them as they stand to a hundred million, and give them another hundred-million nation as neighbors. Change them not at all except to establish them confirmed pacifists. Or make a similar society, all its members altruists, by psychological definition. How long would it be before the cross-sectional activities of their full social living would split and function through conflicting theories and doctrines and verbal idolatries until all mechanisms and techniques at hand would be in use, with who knows what poison's gas for truth's sake.

This is not to attack or jeer at pacifism or altruism. It is only to state their meaning. It is not to scorn a warless world or a world of loving kindness. It is only to describe the characteristic of this one process of striving for it. The meanings of pacifism and altruism are real, not in their verbal claims, but in just that much of our activity which they give expression to: in just that much and no more.

# XVII

## Actor and Environment within the Social Fact

§ 35.  *The Actor-Environment Bifurcation.*   As the position here taken now stands, it may be embodied in the flat assertion that the facts of man-society permit a unified direct statement, which puts them fully before us, and sacrifices nothing either of the man values or of the society values as these may be separately stated.   For the writer this statement rests in his belief that he does so observe them, and that he has been so observing them for twenty-five years with increasing technical satisfaction and with decreasing difficulty from insurgent word-meanings of the older types.

As an argument to others, the emphasis falls on these points.   The matter-mind bifurcation is no longer in any of its forms a hindrance for study to any man familiar with recent types of scientific progress.   The man-society bifurcation is under grave suspicion in the first place because of its patent failure to attain adequate definition for either of its terms in any of many ways in which this has been attempted, whether psychic, socially psychic, or socially environmental.   It is in the second place under suspicion because of the steady trend, specially notable in the culture studies of anthropology, but evident everywhere else in sociology, to get a direct social statement, though still retaining various of the other factors in the outskirts of the study.

So far as this position seems repugnant it will be due to the emphasis on the assertion that a complete statement of the facts can be given in this way. Personally, I should be inclined to attribute such repugnance in any reader to the continuance of undigested word-meanings of the older type in the background of his understanding of what has been said.   I shall approach this situation next by examining a special phase of the man-society bifurcation: the bifurcation, that is, of actor and environment within the social fact.   And again, I shall do it not by analyzing words or discussing current terminologies, but by presenting a typical illustration in this form of statement.

§ 36.   *An Editorial Writer at Work.*   Let us take as our illustration the writing of newspaper editorials.   Here we have something involving knowledges, directions, policies, hidden and open purposes, compensations, ambitions, business connections, and a full net-work of the old style "psychological factors."

Consider an editorial writer upon a large prosperous daily newspaper of the standard commercial type.  Let him, as a side line, write similarly for a pure food magazine with a clientage of fancy-food distributors, consumers of the higher priced foods, and persons with a specialized public-health-diet interest.  Give him a topic on which he sees the arguments on many sides, let us say a pending legislative project covering adulterations of ginger.  Free him from any strong personal judgment or bias; for he surely is as much entitled to be accepted scruple-free as is any pious general commanding in a fierce battle, any druggist selling patent medicines, or any church-going, party-organization candidate for office, 1920 model.  Let him write two articles, one for his newspaper, attacking the proposal; one for his food journal advocating it.

Presented in practical every-day terms, he is a man; with certain ideas, feelings and morals: he writes; he draws his pay; he takes orders; he anticipates orders by sensing what is wanted; he knows the facts, or such of them as he needs; he uses a style, or styles, conformable to those of his papers; he talks with various people with points of view on the subject in hand; he produces articles changing in shading from time to time, or perhaps changing at length in attitude either openly, or else tacitly by the mere process of ceasing to produce on that subject; he has his followers in narrower or wider circle perhaps admiring his style, his logic or his practical sense of what certain conditions require: he has his circle of influence among the readers of his papers: he has his share in the estimated influence of his papers when legislators note their attitudes.

§ 37. *Examined under the Euclidean Space Form.* All of this presents itself in space: there is no doubt of that. But in the ordinary statements it presents itself under the dominance of the Euclidean space form in every element of its statement, which is a very different matter. Consider what it means. The frame of reference used by mathematicians in Euclidean space is three straight lines intersecting at one point, each perpendicular to the others, like the lines of wall and ceiling intersection in one corner of a square room, idealized as absolutely true. Planes on these lines and planes parallel to them divide all space into cubic units. If the foot is the standard measure, then all space is present in a great number of exact cubic feet fitting perfectly to one another.

Put our editorial writer and his activities in this space. His head is in one cubic foot, his body in certain other cubic feet adjacent, his typewriter in another one near by, his editorial supervision in certain cubic feet not far away, his printing presses in still others, and his readers in still others. His behavior is in space at any rate, even though we have our private ideas as to where his mind may be under the terms of the old puzzle split. But at any rate if he has his mind and another man his, then they present themselves in different parts of that space, and their relation to one another is across that space.

This is not only the common every-day statement of him, but it is the basis of the sociologies prior to Einstein. It is at the basis of all the confusions of individual mind and social mind, individual psychology and social psychology. There is certainly nothing wrong about it as far as it goes. The trouble with it is in the interpretation of society where it makes all the problems insoluble.

§ 38. *The Puzzles under Such Examination.* What are some of these insoluble problems?

One is cause and effect across this space, psychic and material impingement. This is now flatly unscientific in the sense that all scientific progress has been in the elimination of problems of that type.

Another is the locus in space of the specified and often personified products of the activity, in this

case the law and the editorial policy.  Of that we
have already treated.

The third which is now to examine is actor and
environment in this field of psychic description
within the social fact, a bifurcation assumed when
the study is made from the point of view of behavior,
but which our study must make not from that point
of view, but from the point of view of law and policy
as socially present.

§ 39.  *Examined as Man-Society Activity.*  Now
if one will refer to the description of the editorial
writer's activity in section 36, it seems to me that
everything there listed except the specification "a
man with certain ideas, feelings and morals, who
writes" is capable of statement as a fact of observation only across several or many lives.  The ex-
cepted specification stands out as individual in its
terms.  But nevertheless even this, so far as it
bears on the editorial writing activity must be
stated within it, that is socially.  The "man with
certain ideas, feelings and morals, who writes" is
of course, also specified for many other activities,
at the intersection of which, according to the present
theory, he gets his standing, naming and description
as such a man.  The point for us at this immediate
moment, however, is not whether the whole of the
man will have been described when all of the man-

society activities have been described, but technically and exactly what the description is in this particular activity whether of the man as actor in a social environment, or directly in terms of a man-society activity to which this actor-environment split is for the purposes in hand an irrelevant distinction.

Under the actor-environment statement our emphasis is on "John Smith," the editorial writer, who "writes" "an editorial" under such and such "direction" for "such and such a number of individual readers," with each factor so emphasized taken as capable of independent definition prior to the attempt at interpretative relation.

Under the activity statement our emphasis will be on certain food purveying activity, netted with other food purveying activities, under certain specifications of purity and impurity, and certain substitutions of impurity for purity and the reverse, reacted on partly by purveyors and partly by consumers to give dominance to the purity specification or the reverse, using a series of representative governmental processes, and represented in the journalistic process by certain language specifications, these appearing from the typewriter of John Smith and the presses of the newspaper and magazine proprietors (who now present themselves as loci of phenomena examined, not as unit facts) and passing across this or that reading public (these publics again as loci of investigation). The interpretation here is in terms of the activities each in respect to the others.

§ 40. *Further Details of the Writing Process.* Common practical remarks about John Smith are that he is an expert or awkward writer, that he is a good or bad journalist, that he has a flair, a touch, perhaps an instinct. The reader who does not like what he writes will call him a fool or a knave. The one who does like it will say: "Oh, noble judge; oh, excellent young man." The feebleness of these practical comments when taken up into careful interpretation is apparent. And the point at issue is that it is just such practical comments, which are so taken up and which are continued for interpretative use by an attempt to clarify and refine them.

Consider some of these points. What about the flair? John Smith has it and as a result he needs very little direction. Let the proprietor or his personal representative be absent, and John Smith will not vary far from the track. Therefore he is a "good" journalist and not a "bad" one. But the "bad" man in the place also has his flair. It happens to be for other social activities and expressions. The wrong things for the particular purpose in hand are expressing themselves in him, and in his case as in John Smith's those are social activities in their networks.

How about the very wordings he used which make his expertness for the particular writing he is doing. Suppose he cleverly shades a word meaning. He may say that "he" got the shading himself or out of himself. But apart from the posited "he," and the posited "himself," which no student pretends to understand very well, and which can only be used in social interpretation by dragging them in as if they were understood in advance, we do have enough knowledge of that field which the psycho-analyst calls the unconscious to justify us in saying that "he" may not know at all where he got it, and yet have got it very definitely at some particular time and place. A glance of his eye at a word on a page, when something very different was before him, may have garnered it.

§ 41. *Comparison from Psycho-Analysis.* I fear I am repeating on this point to weariness. But nothing is more common than for the response to be: "Of course, that is all true; it is obvious and indeed commonplace": and yet for such surface agreement to let the whole mass of similar interpretative factors survive all around, and continually recur with their feeble pretenses of explaining events.

The question is not whether there are little changes

or even great changes of expression as the various
social activities pass through the various men, but
instead how we trace down these changes to explain
them.   It is not whether John Smith fits in one
place in the activities, or John Jones in another,
but instead the very description of all the John
Smiths and John Joneses in all the activities borne
by them.

Consider what psycho-analysis has done in broad-
ening our understandings of the specific positions—
behaviors—of individuals in man-society.   It has
gone beyond the immediate durations and immediate space contacts, and spread out the interpretations far and long.   It is fearsomely concrete in its
statement of the individual, even though, or perhaps rather because, it adds his concrete sub-conscious to his previous concrete conscious description.
It is inclined when it gets interested in society
around the man, to carry up its extended concrete
individual into explanations that become ludicrous
to almost every reader of them.   All that does not
matter: it is scaffolding or by-play.   The important
thing is what it does in the hospital and the clinic,
by adding more and wider facts to the first observations.   All its facts are social activity facts, and it
is not improper to bring its widenings of observation
into comparison with the widenings that have been

going on in the last generation of study of society
and that are insisted on for their full scope and meaning here.

§ 42.  *The Personification of Man-Society Activities.*  Our old habit has been to personify the Man.
A newer effort has been to personify the Society,
the Social Whole or the Social Mind.  If we feel compelled, because of any of our established contacts
with some of the phases of the man-society process
that enfolds us, to personify anything, we might
just as well and just as successfully personify the
cross-sectional activities.  This has indeed been
occasionally tried, as with Sovereignty.  What it
helps us I do not know.  Positing the reality of a
grammatical subject is about all it provides.  Much
better hold our material fluid as it is.  The clottings
of activities, to which reference will be made in a
later chapter may seem to ask for some such personification, but even with them it is a hindrance to
knowledge, not a help.

§ 43.  *The Audience-Writer Activity.*  Actor-environment in the material we have just been going over
presents itself as a complex of subject-matter, writer,
audience.  Passing over the subject-matter and
writer situation as simpler and more clearly evident,
let us take actor-environment in the writer-audience
situation to emphasize the unit fact of observation.

John Smith we say in current fashion, knows his audience; (the word audience being used in fault of a better to cover his readers, his public, and not merely hearers).  That is only to refer crudely to the man-society fact that writer-audience are one activity.  Audience influences writer we say.  That is only to state crudely what can be much more exactly expressed by saying that audience-writer activity is one.  I prefer to assert flatly that no writing is done in which the audience or audiences in this sense are not active.  This covers the Ten Commandments on Sinai, and the last trivial comment of the day.  Every writer in a professional way knows exactly what fact is here meant, no matter how he expresses it.  Every writer of any kind and in any place knows it or can recognize it, unless perhaps he has swathed himself in personal dignity and self-idolatry to hide it.  There is no complaint against any other way of describing it a man may want for his purpose.  All are free.  But this is the description which fits the study of man-society to the last detail.

# XVIII

## Human Nature as Environment

§ 44. *Description in Terms of Individuals Not Contrasted with Description in Terms of Man-Society, but Rather an Experiment within the Possibilities of the Latter.* The preceding chapter asserts that even the most subtle shadings of opinion can be stated directly as representative activity through and across the individuals with more accuracy than they can be stated in terms of individuals or their qualities. A form of statement representative of this assertion structurally might be: The actor and his environment are offered to us by habitual customary phrasing as appearing under space forms, though with certain features (the psychic) not existing in space, while nevertheless manifesting themselves only in space: this very space and all the distinctions of actors and environments within it being nevertheless observational presentations of the very process, the description of which it pretends to control.

We are not changing the emphasis of either of the above statements very much when we put it as follows. The current description of social happenings in terms of individual men and their psychic qualities has no precedence on the face of it over any other kind of description. The individual with his psychic qualities is no reality contrasted to other realities, but he is simply a verbal technique of stating observations for practical purposes. The individual and all the psychic is a social method of description and stands or falls like all other methods of description through its functioning representative value. Interpretation in terms of individuals is not the eternal enemy of all other forms of interpretation, but merely a candidate for adoption, along with many other candidates, within the general man-society interpretative process.

We have thus far been proceeding by an effort to make direct man-society statements of material offered us, crowding the individual backward as much as we can here and there, mentioning him in incidental arguments. It is now time, however, to change this procedure somewhat, and examine the facts rather from the point of view of the individual himself. Attention may be given to such points of approach as human nature, instincts and the individual as the standard of measurement.

§ 45. *Typical Implications of Human Nature.*
Common conceptions of human nature are comparable to the old ideas of space and time in the
tough and obstructive clottings that they interpose
to the thorough study of man-society facts; whether
in the guise of individual human nature or of racial human nature. Unlike the psychological student of human nature who admits that he does not understand it
at all, but is only working at it, the sociological
investigator is apt to take it over as if he understood it at least enough for his purpose. He takes
it as if it were certainly there, and bound to remain
still "individual human nature" no matter how
much more understanding of it analysis gives. He
takes it, that is, not as a descriptive term for his
facts, as the psychologist does, but as a factor to
use in explaining other facts which he separates
from it. He determines its value in advance, in
general, if not in specific detail. And therefore it
becomes for him the dumping ground of all his more
troublesome problems.

What are the typical implications of human
nature, as the term is thus commonly used? It
characterizes an assumed end term in cosmic evolution, man. It indicates the assumed highest values
in that evolution series—our own as individuals. It
gives a locus for the mind side of the mind-matter

bifurcation. It contains a reduction into terms of individual men of as much of the observed procedure of man-society as can possibly be forced into such a form of statement.

Combining these implications we may say that human nature, in common acceptance, values itself as the highest development in the physical series, specifies within itself as much of society as it can crowd into its meanings, takes over naïvely the mind-matter, conscious-unconscious, actor-environment, man-society bifurcations, and nevertheless claims to be a definite reality in terms of which man-society can be explained.

§ 46. *Reject from It the Social Content.* The first step in clearing up this confusion is manifestly to sweep out of it all of the forms of social activity that are specified or implied in it. They are our problems, and are not at all solved when we present the same thing on one side in terms of an individual to explain the same thing on the other side in terms of society. If we are able to state the facts at all as activities then we are required to put that description through to the bitter end, before we pass judgment on its value.

§ 47. *Separate Its Psychological Statement.* The next step is to separate the points of view of psychology and man-society. If psychology rests on a postulated split of actor and environment, as we have seen that it frankly does in its most definite development, the study of behavior, then clearly the psychological approach cannot come over directly into a study that must necessarily begin by postulating no such split. What has been learned of process in man-society by a study under the postulated split must be fully known and allowed for by the student who proceeds on the rejection of that split, but it cannot demand to be taken up bodily by him in its own terms.

§ 48. *Instincts as Pseudo-Psychic Connecting Links*. What now have we left? Perhaps instincts. Now as a matter of fact, the interpretative contribution of psychology to sociology which once included everything up to ideas and ideals and moral judgments, has been gradually narrowed down until often it includes nothing but instincts; and moreover the instincts, once stated as very numerous and very definite, have been progressively generalized and reduced in number, until now in the writers who build most solidly upon them they appear maybe as half a dozen or a dozen, with of course no agreement in any two writers as to which particular instincts should be listed and which not. Further this tendency has a trend of development already evident, to reduce the instinct factor to just one item. What is this one item? The answer is plain when we examine what these instincts are from a man-society point of view.

The instinct as we find it seems to be a statement that the physical organism as it stands in the evolutionary series, seems to act just so. But instead of stating this as a generalization of the organism, it is stated in what purports to be a psychic or pseudo-psychic term, namely instinct. And why? So as to give it flexibility when its specific usage makes trouble. Not functioning flexibility, but problem-dodging flexibility. In short it points to a mode of activity, which seems to want a statement somewhere between the social and the organic, and this statement is made psychic, the instinct. Now if we generalize the instincts to one, we have simply living activity, the going process of the organism, its urge, push, energy. Which may very well be accepted; but which cannot be used in interpretation.

§ 49. *Instincts as Environment.* How is it with sex and nutrition in society? As physiology they have their description in Euclidean space, barring what trouble may come for this from the electrical interpretations, and not to mention the Bohr orbits. As individual experience they have first approximations to statement in that generalized everyday space form. Technically in psychology they have statements on the basis of actor-environment behavior. Socially they are beyond that. The posited connecting-link, instinct, helps nothing.

I do not hesitate to say that when we break down the obscurities of this connecting-link, and when we have made our statement of man-society activities, covering sex and nutrition phenomena as they appear there, the remaining content of the term instinct will present itself to the sociological activity statement as environment in much the same sense that a coal mine, a river, a farm horse, a fertile field, or a gas engine now presents itself. As such environment, in varying degrees at the varying stages of the investigation for its varying purposes, it may be projected, with the qualifications that at some other stage under other purpose, it must itself be taken as within the social activity, like all other environment down to the last stage, as Einstein has proved to us, the environmental space and time.

§ 50. *A Speculative Interlude.* As an interlude, a speculative observation from the limitational background is desirable. Does this characteristic of comprehensiveness or inclusiveness, this union of actor-environment in a cross sectional activity background mark a break between the study of man-society and other phenomena? Not at all. Repro-

duction in all its later forms has its two-in-oneness
in something of this sense.  Disease variations in
terms of aggregations of animals have their reference.  Molecules and atoms even now make their
contribution.  Every genetic chart tells the story.

Animal societies require cross sectional statement
for the reported observations upon them to have any
meaning.  Does some one announce that his tests
show an ant will die of solitude alone?  Whether
verified or not, and no matter how it can be traced
down physiologically if true, it has its aspect that
requires this statement.  If one will listen for a
few years to the modulations of expression of a
casual flock of hens, not with some vain effort to
understand them, but merely to note how much is
indicated beyond our present ability to label, he
will distrust any statement in terms of separate
hens.

Speculation, of course, with no direct value.
Useful merely to warn us against imagining a series
of physical separates right up to where man-society
begins.

§ 51.  *Further Illustration.*  A final illustration from
the use of tobacco or drugs, called socially a custom,
individually a habit.  Cross-sectional and representative are all judgments of the effects, whether bad
or good, down to the latest pathological study.  The

smoker reports himself to us in personal terms of his own life. He cannot avoid his craving, or he can let it alone. But his "can" and "cannot" become social when analyzed. We know what the quasi-medical cures have amounted to. We know what necessity may bring. Some protracted observations of a smoker, both in his abstinences and addictions, and likewise in his transitional periods, leave me no fear but what the full statement may be made in cross-sectional representative terms, with all that is referred to as factors of human nature standing environmental to it in the same sense and no other than are pipe and tobacco, cigar or cigarette.

Take instead of tobacco user, the drug addict, the user of cocaine or whatever drug may be worse from the pathologist's viewpoint. The extent of the social statement in terms of discovery and supply, and of favoring and unfavoring "social environments" as that term is often used in reference to the individual is well enough known. The physiologist's report will contain nothing to destroy the report in terms of man-society, no matter what disease terms he may use, no matter what he may tell us of deteriorated tissue, or infer about degeneration, eugenics or stock.

§ 52. *The Individual as Standard of Measurement or Values.* Of the individual man as a standard of values in the social sciences, very little need be said in addition to what evidently follows from the preceding discussion.   If the very definition of the individual arises in the man-society processes of activity, it is certainly far-fetched to take that individual so defined and make out of him a test for judging the process.   And all the more so since the slightest inspection shows that any individual so used is not an individual in general, but a highly specified individual, the full specification coming from the social activities for the particular purposes defined in them at each stage of the process.

The individual man may also be taken as a standard of measurement more widely than is usually meant when we speak of a standard of values.   A straight psychological interpretation of society facts aims in this direction.   What success any other worker may have on this line is not for me to say. Who attempts it must cope both with the established relativity of physics and the many apparent relativities of society, and work within their frame; or else he must overthrow the former and attain exact interpretation of all the latter.   It is a fair field for whoever desires the adventure.

# XIX

## Differences Between Men: Birth and Death

§ 53. *Differences Between Races.* A distinguished anthropologist said recently that so far as intelligence, capacity, went, there was little difference between a Cro-Magnon and a modern man. A distinguished psychologist says that if one should take an infant of the time of Tut-ankh-amen, transport him to America and educate him at Harvard, his chances of academic success would probably be the same as those of the average young man born today. Investigations are indicating more and more clearly all the time that the mean level of intelligence has only very slight, if any, differences, between the different races, peoples or tribes whose cultures can be examined by us, and that these differences are if anything more in temporary specializations of capacity than in any positive higher or lower, more or less.

At the same time there are very great differences,

at least in our first descriptions and probably in our final descriptions, between different cultures and civilizations, in degree of complexity, in emphasis of predominant types of activity, in technique and other aspects.

In view of the reports of biologist, anthropologist and psychologist the sociologist is manifestly barred from starting his interpretations with any confidence that differences in intelligence or other capacities between different races or other groups, will be a fundamental factor in explaining differences in civilizations.

§ 54. *Differences between Individuals.* How is it as regards differences between individual men inside a single society considered as factors of explanation? Not a whit better.

Heroes are most interesting to contemplate, but what does hero-worship do? It takes a social situation at a social valuation, identifies it with an individual, and builds up a statement of it in individual capacities unified into a personality. The result may be most convincing and interesting and inspiring, but that has no importance in social interpretation. The only test here is how far can it be universalized.

Heroizing in all its forms from obscure attitude to blind devotion, and from personal relation to high

flights of literature, is cross sectional representative activity, and therefore fact for sociology.    But
as a component of social interpretation, note its
assumptions.

Personality is an assumption, most doubtful where
most carefully studied.    The same with capacities.
The social situation in which the hero is given dominant description is a fact, but the social valuation
of it as a great fact is only another fact of a representative nature made in a special limited durational
setting.    We receive from it only a set of facts, in
a special verbal statement, presenting itself with
color of authority only by absolutizing its words so
as to obscure the problems, rather than by functioning them so as to open up the problems.

And what is true of heroizing on the great scale
is true of everything akin to it, down to heroizing—
individualizing for interpretative purposes—the least
spectacular of the actors.

§ 55.    *Variety in Individuals.*    Yet how various
are our individuals, in description as persons, in
identification with social activity and achievement,
in attainment of rewards.    One can go to a strange
city of five millions in his own country, and not con-
fuse any two individuals.    If one goes to a strange
nation of a hundred millions, and fails in this identification of individuals—if all people look alike to him

—all Chinese to an American or all Americans to a Chinese—it is only the observer's specialized aptitude to his own type of facial expressions, that hampers him, not a greater degree of likeness in the foreign individuals.

What is true of expression of facts is true of bumps on the head, of the carriage of the clothed body, of the voice. On a country telephone line with perhaps several thousand users, acquaintances never think of introducing themselves by name. With all this material, however, phrenologies, whether of bumps, of cranial formations, or of facial expressions, have little place outside of short stories, where they answer for facile pictorial tags to connect writer and readers vividly.

§ 56. *Physical Tests of Individuals*. Temperaments, inventive genius, specialized chess playing capacity, mathematical ability, artistic ability, musical ability and all the others are describable. No two individuals are alike. A heart specialist can tell us within reasonable limits of certainty whether a runner can complete his course or will drop dead on the route. An army intelligence test may indicate with somewhat smaller probabilities of accuracy what special portions of the great activity the individual will fit into with free function. Other intelligence tests for other lines of activity in peace time may have certain values in result to be worked out in experience.

But none of them help explain the social activities, their presence, their connections, their survivals and dominations.   The tested individual is socially specialized before he is tested, and who can say how much of the test applies to extra-social capacity and how much to adaptation already accomplished. The mathematical genius is a genius in terms of his output in a given social situation, but who can say in last analysis, what minute specialization of function in some minute portion of his brain lets him— and not some other man—be there in that particular situation?   Who can tell how many other men, hundreds or thousands perhaps in his own day, millions perhaps in the long series of man-society observations, have had a similar specialization, without the social situation to function it in.   The cretin is to modern science no longer baldly an idiot—a complete bad personality—but just a perfectly good possible person barring a thyroid deficiency.   Glands, hormones, these, are the meaningful terms in which this whole side of man-society is being interpreted. They do not give the explanation of man-society, which sociology today must use.   They give us a limit, a changing limit, somewhere off in the distance, with which a long time from now sociology

must perhaps make its definite contacts and adjustments.

In short physiology and pathology tell us something about what individual is here and what there
in social activity today, but they have no touch at
all with what social activity is here and what there
today.

§ 57.  *Birth and Death.*  The generalization of this
whole side of the problem puts itself best of all in
simple terms of birth and death.  Not that birth
and death are simple by any means.  They are the
complicated field of the physical-physiological series
of interpretations.

The student of man-society must not be taken as
denying birth and death of individuals, nor any of
the accompanying life-span facts of individuals,
when he sets them aside and begins his work and
pushes his interpretations in social activities direct.
He is simply recognizing his field, and recognizing
the non-functioning words that are so often used in
connection with it, and insisting that the terminology
of his own field be a functioning problem-analyzing
terminology, and not an obscure problem-concealing
terminology.

# XX

## Simmel: Durkheim: Ratzenhofer

§ 58. *The Search for Observational Coherence in Social Facts.* Apart from compilers of materials and formal systematizers, whose work is of lesser order, it seems to me that the three great names of modern sociology are Simmel, Durkheim and Ratzenhofer. All three of them were independent investigators with a powerful control of material; but the characteristic that unites them and makes them stand out together from all others is their determined struggle to reveal in that material what is its peculiarly and truly social content. Unlike the facile writers of many well-known texts and systems they were none of them content to add potatoes to loving kindness, or buttermilk to religion, in the glib hope that this peculiar x plus y would make an intelligible z.

The three men differ much, it is true, in the deliberateness with which they face this question of the peculiarly social, and they differ much in the character of their separate investigations and contributions. They are very far apart indeed in the psychological and methodological foundations they give their systems. But as one of them, Simmel, has said: "It is indeed true in matters of the mind and spirit that what we so commonly call fundamental is often less firm and solid than the structure erected above it: and for the widest and most difficult problems one may even say that this is always true."

It is not then in their scaffoldings, whether of psychology or metaphysics, nor by any eclectic process, that I shall attempt to unite these men, but rather by striving to show that in the one great essential, the direct visioning of social facts, there is substantial agreement: an agreement that in the old space and time world might well be overlooked, but that in the new world of physics is easy to trace. This quality they have in common, this characteristic which they have sought in society, we cannot call it objectivity—the word is one-sided: nor can we call it positivity—the word is too vague: perhaps for the moment we may call it observational coherence in the material, the social facts, permitting a unified study of it in its own right.

§ 59.   *Ratzenhofer's Groups and Interests.*   Ratzenhofer's contribution is the systematic working out of social evolution and social process in terms of groups of men interacting on each other as groups, rather than as individuals. This group process which he uses we may describe, for lack of a better word, as comparatively concrete. That is, he takes his groups, in a first approximation, as so and so many men functioning together. Ludwig Gumplowicz had preceded Ratzenhofer with his Rassenkampf, which was primarily a theory of the origin of society in tribal warfare and its development through further race struggle. For both men the background was of course Austria with its race conflicts. Where Gumplowicz, much more concretely still, had seen separate hordes or tribes or races grinding together, Ratzenhofer advanced to describing a similar functional process in all large social operations within a society, including political parties, and beyond to various somewhat hypothetical structures of civilization. His classification of these large social operations though derived from Schäffle and Spencer, was carefully developed by him in terms of the society around him.

Underlying each such social operation, whether large or small, he placed what he called an "Interest." For our view here, his great merit is that this Interest, this system of Interests, though psychologically stated, comes down in practice to be merely another form of statement for the active procedure of the group and system of groups, a form of statement that emphasized the living activity side, without entanglement with individual psychological factors taken as direct factors of interpretation. For him therefore all the energy aspects of the social facts lie directly within those social facts as such and are not imported to them from outside.

Ratzenhofer felt the need of wide systematizing discussion of his material in connection with all the materials of other sciences; he felt the need of working out a "positive monism" to underly his sociology. He gave many long years of study to this. His positive monism, however interesting it was, is now only part of the history of an older type of science. His systematic construction cannot last any more than any systematic sociologies of today can last. More striking discoveries than the tomb of Tut-ankh-amen, or the Mongolian nest of ten million year old dinosaur eggs are to be found in the sphere of man-society; and present systematic constructions must all stand ready for radical alteration from decade to decade, if not from year to year.

The credit to Ratzenhofer is for his group process, his visioning of it as activity involving its own energy, which he stated in terms of social interests, and his refusal to let any other kind of psychic factor distort his work or stop it from going as far as his power in his own day would take it.

§ 60. *Durkheim's Exteriority and Constraint.* With Durkheim who rejected systematizations as impracticable for the present, we get a closer and more intimate view of the man-society process. But at the same time we have it presented to us as over and against a posited individual. The energy appears as the constraint which this exterior society imposes upon the individual.

His viewpoint may be compressed into the following sentences. The social fact is a social thing (chose). It is characterized by being exterior to the individual consciousness. And again by exercising constraint upon the individual consciousness. Social facts must be explained only by other social facts, and never by reference to individual psychologic facts.

His personal investigations were into the division of labor in society with emphasis upon such factors as the volume and density of the society, into suicide as a social fact amenable to social control: and into the characteristics of the religious life as shown in its earliest forms. Under his influence his school has produced many works of great interest and importance.

As he progressed he elaborated a psychology, both

individual and social, to provide him his background, his contact with the rest of science. This psychology posits a social mind on the analogy of individual minds, but more vivid, more real than individual minds. Most psychic content is for him described as in the social mind, very little as in the individual mind. In pursuance of such study he has tried to show how the concepts of space and time and force are socially constructed, and with them all other social concepts, thus setting forth what has been called a sociological theory of knowledge. Some of his followers have carried this treatment still farther, one of them, for example, arguing that memory is itself socially produced. As with Ratzenhofer we may strip away his scaffolding of social mind and psychology, and hold to the working meanings of his description of the social fact, these being his true scientific delivery to us.

Durkheim gives us then this. The social fact is something for scientific study in its own direct description. His terms exteriority and constraint serve to indicate this directness and immediacy of the social fact, though we would use other terms today because we do not need any longer to set it off over and against an individual consciousness posited as observing it and being affected by it. The meaning of each phase of social fact must be sought in other phases of social fact, and along with meanings, all references, forces, values. He gives us this not as a dictum, but in large results by the use of his method.

§ 61. *Simmel's Forms.* Pass now to Simmel, again as with the others, to take from him, not any features of his philosophy or incidental attitudes, but to secure his working attitude as perhaps the keenest and most searching investigator society has yet had, undoubtedly the one with the greatest yield of permanently applicable knowledge. With society concretely in the sense of a mass of men here and a mass there as Ratzenhofer looked at it Simmel has little concern. With Durkheim's opposition to the posited individual he has no concern at all. But he is vastly more intimate, more subtle, than any other investigator has been, in catching the inter-influencings of social men. He seeks that which is peculiarly social in society (Vergesellschaftung). His separation is between the content and the form in society. The form is what he studies.

The form is what is peculiarly social. And these remarkable studies he has made of social form are what seem to me to contain today our most thoroughly secure knowledge of society. Superiority and subordination, competition, imitation, division of labor, party formation, class formation, representation, the ones, the twos, the threes and the manys, inner and outer determination, compared as they appear in this country or that, in this kind of process (economic, religious, political, etc.) or that, with respect to the influence of numbers, size of the society, with respect to secrecy or publicity, or in a thousand other aspects. His largest single study, that of money, concerns itself not merely with value and material in economic service, but with all the connections of money in its various forms with religion, science, art, public life, personal freedom and type of culture.

His own foundation of psychology is much more exact than that of either Ratzenhofer or Durkheim, but by its very clarity it brings out its values for ready judgment under the new science which has arisen since Simmel's death. All the material of both psychological and sociological study, he holds, is psychic. Looked at by psychology it is all individual psychology: though within this individual psychology we may mark off, if we wish, a special limited portion which we may call social psychology, namely that part which deals with the technique of the influencing of one individual by another under social conditions. But when the same material is looked at by sociology, where content and configuration of the psychic facts is in question, we find our facts vastly transcending the individual. State, law, religion, morals, run far beyond the individual in any definition we can give them. Yet they do not need a psychic bearer, a social mind, a social person. They are facts, social facts, to be taken as such and studied in their social forms, the network of these forms giving us the science of sociology.

One thing Simmel seems to lack, the forcefulness, the energy, pointed to by Ratzenhofer's interests, by Durkheim's exterior constraint. One only weakness he seems to have, and this he brings out so clearly himself that a hunt for criticism is needless. His forms he compares frequently to form in geometry, in Euclid. He uses the illustration so frequently that he may perhaps be said to have justified his search for social forms by analogies with geometric forms. Today, however, when Euclidean geometry is absorbed into physics, for Simmel's sociology what is manifestly needed is that its statement too should pass into one of energy, of activity, or of interests or pressures, if those last terms happen to be used without false meanings. In his day-book, found after his death, Simmel had written, "I shall die without heirs of the spirit. So be it." But he has left us nevertheless the greatest heritage of all.

§ 62. *The Unity of Viewpoint when Doubtful Foundation Systems are Stripped Away.* One cannot make a synthesis of selected elements from the life work of these three men. Much less can one combine their underlying philosophical structures. But one has no need of those underlying structures, the least important part, as Simmel said, of all difficult investigations, in order to see their likeness in point of view toward what really is of importance, the handling of the social facts themselves.

Ratzenhofer gave us the groups of men in terms of interests, now appearing as definable activities across society. Durkheim gave us the independence and forcefulness of the social facts, which we need no longer contract to a posited individual. Simmel made the intimate study of the forms of activity, lacking just the little touch of groupal forcefulness which falls to it simply, inevitably, from the new physical science since Einstein. There we have in very truth the appearing sociology, coherent in its own field.

§ 63. *An Indication from Studies of Culture.* Does it seem unfair to select these three men for praise in this way, ignoring elements in their work that have been criticized in the work of others (as for example Durkheim's occasional slippings into use of factors from individual psychology, which theoretically he contemned); while at the same time failing to recognize strivings similar to theirs in many investigators, and failing at the same time to bring into account all the great progress through three generations towards direct social statement, upon the basis of which they did their work? It is not here a question of merit or reward or fame, but only of the valuation of achievements in sociological investigation as it is before us today. I have no doubt but that the great majority of investigators of society have longed and striven for the same unified vision of social fact, the same coherence of observation. The difference is that these three have done their great work under continuing standards of such coherence. No others have pressed so hard, nor with such success towards the goal.

For that field of anthropological study known as culture, a word, however, should be said. Here in the description of the facts we find more progress, more unity than anywhere else. Several recent works attain a very great unity of statement, and one can almost see in every case of a slipping towards other interpretation that it comes in at a point merely where information fails. It serves to tide over a bad moment. But none of these works venture directly into the theoretical field which is here in question.

# XXI

## Typical Attempts at Classification of Groups

§ 64. *General Terms Used in Classifications.* Village, town, county, province, state, is a series of terms, which along with many others similar, describes assemblages of men within exact territorial limits, on a basis comprehensive of all men within those territorial limits (barring, perhaps, or perhaps not, travellers through them and temporary residents).

Horde is a term similarly comprehensive of all men within certain territorial limits, but with this territory movable. In certain usages for early society family and tribe are akin to it in this respect.

Family, clan, tribe, caste, estate, are terms descriptive commonly of groups of men on such basis that each man belongs to one unit and one only of the particular type, without the unit having its precise and unbroken territory. As, for instance, among the clans, each man belongs to one clan, and one only, and all the clans with all their members, though without separate geographical districts, make up the members of the larger body, say nation, which has its geographical district.

Community, class, group, are terms of somewhat more general meaning, leading to classifications in which not only the geographical classification breaks down, but also the membership in terms of full and complete personal identification tends to disappear.

We have then pre-sociological terms offered to sociological theory grouping men (1) by definite or shifting territorial limits, (2) by definite personal adherence with an interpenetration of territorial spread, and (3) by activities which drop the complete personal specification as well as the complete territorial specification. The terms all seem definite enough before used by sociologists, but the attempt to fixate them for theoretical purposes develops vaguenesses. Various writers have their various usages, determined largely by the particular emphasis on various aspects which his own special study requires. We may say of all of them that wherever there is reduction to genetic or even geographical factors as final criterion of classification there is a weakness. The real classification is of man-activity, groupal, cross sectional; and the geographical and genetic factors, however prominent in this case or in that, are faulty, so long as they are regarded as outside the activity and not taken up into it, in its terms.

§ 65. *Some Recent Examples of Classification.* Without delaying to examine any of the sweeping classifications, whether racial, political, industrial, anatomical or pathological, we may note that there has recently been an increasing tendency to gain finer discrimination between group-activity types; and we may inspect briefly the criteria used in a few cases with an eye to their practical value.

Charles Horton Cooley led the way in this country by distinguishing "primary" or "face-to-face" groups from all others; and while I have not observed that he himself used the term "secondary" for other forms that he contrasted with them, such as "types," "classes" and "institutions," his followers commonly refer to him as if he had. But Cooley's real interest lay in the "primary ideals" which he located within these primary groups. Ellwood in his various discussions always begins with the "face-to-face" groups; after which he draws distinctions between involuntary and voluntary groups, the former being natural or genetic, and the latter purposive or interest groups; or between sanctioned and unsanctioned groups, the former being institutional. Ellwood's interest, however, is never in exact analysis but in broad general descriptions.

Maciver puts all of his work into a structure of classification using primarily two terms, community and association. Community is "any whole area of social life such as a village or town or country." Association is "an organization of social beings for the pursuit of some common interest or interests. It is a determinate social unity built upon common purpose." The state is "a peculiarly authoritative association within community." The great law of communal development is that "socialization and individualization are the two sides of a single process." Without permitting himself to be too definite in anything Maciver connects volitional social operations with non-geographical organization, and he stresses questions of personality over all others in his theory. No matter how interesting his books may be to read from special points of view, we make little advance towards social interpretation in this way.

McDougall, first rejecting from his consideration the fortuitous and ephemeral groups, divides all others into two divisions, natural and artificial. The natural groups divide into those rooted in kinship and those determined by geographical considerations. The artificial groups fall into three classes: purposive, customary or traditional, and mixed.

Here again we have geographical and racial distinctions, and differences as to volition in organization, as the tests for classification.

Several attempts to handle this problem of classification from a professedly philosophical point of view have recently appeared in the periodicals. Following Boodin, Wieman uses personality for his clue, distinguishing between personal and impersonal groups. "In the personal group," he says, "the response of the members to one another involves the entire personality both as subject and object of response: its order is highly plastic and its personnel is permanent. In the impersonal group the response of the members to one another involves the minimum of personality both as subject and as object: its order is rigid and its personnel is transitory." But Wieman frankly admits that no actual group is ever either personal or impersonal, and that all actual groups are "a mixture of these two types."

Another attempt, by Pepper, gives us a classification into concentric or hierarchical groups (or societies, as he calls them), and intersectional groups. The former are activities like government or army, arranged in stages, in which, he asserts, each higher stage has authority over each lower. The intersectional groups are found within the concentric, but "the purposes about which they are formed are

not means to the purposes of the system." This
has an appearance of definiteness but it will not
hold up for a moment when applied to any concrete
bit of society, such as, let us say, any complete
governing activity. Moreover it is set in, and gets
all its meanings out of, a "working definition" of
society as "a unity constituted by the purposeful
activity of living organisms for the mutual benefit
of one another," in which the "individuals," their
separate "lives," their "purposeful" action, and the
"mutual benefit" are stressed as independent determining facts.

For the most part these definitions are hardly
worth quoting except to show how erratic are the
paths of men lost in a verbal fog. Perry's careful
analysis of the great variety of meanings for such
words as personal and impersonal should be taken
into account by any one attempting classifications
by this or similar tests. Holding that society is
not a person in any properly defined sense, Perry
speculates on the possibilities of impersonal groups
constituted of impersonal members, a personal society composed of non-persons, and an impersonal
society composed of persons; and while putting all
stress on the last shows the possibility of the others
as organization forms. Under his definite meaning
for personality he secures a general principle that

"the personality of the whole is inversely proportional to that of its members." His particular problem of personality, however, has become one that no longer interferes with such studies of man in society as the present work advocates, though, of course, it shows no tendency towards them.

§ 66.  *Tönnies.*  One will find running through all these and similar classifications of groups, along with the geographical and racial factors, more or less emphasized or subordinated, the two struggling pseudo-criteria of classification, habitual or volitional, personal or impersonal.  And this no matter how the phrasing runs.  Tönnies as early as 1887 had discussed, in his volume *Gemeinschaft und Gesellschaft*, community and society, the deep organic unity of men on the one side, and the artificial, mechanical or volitional organization on the other: and had given this distinction a psychological foundation (of the objective psychic type) in an elaborate theory of Wesenwille and Willkühr (later called by him Kürwille).  The social fact contrast, the institutional opposition, upon which he was resting, derived through Spencer from Sir Henry Maine.  On the one side Tönnies sees social situations accepted (bejaht) by the individual for their own sake, even though with some sense of their values and purposes; on the other he sees social situations accepted purely as means to recognized ends; on the one side the individuals feel themselves members of a real whole, a Gemeinschaft; on the other the individuals form a system of persons with a fictive Gesellschaft.  On the one side will is objective, naturally grown up and bound with thought; on the other side it is subjective, something produced around and through thought.  Little in the attempts I have mentioned or any other similar ones I know of, has any theoretical value beyond Tönnies' proposals.

§ 67.  *Externality of Common Criteria.*  Beyond question most of these efforts at classification satisfy certain values of the workers who advance them and of others who join with them or follow them. But that is not the question for the general body of social investigation.  The geographical and genetic efforts are in many cases almost right, almost assimilated with the material of social activity to be handled, but the personal and volitional efforts seem to me entirely outside the case.  The very fact that with the huge amount of attention going to social study, they none of them enter definitely and by general consent into its professional handling is evidence enough.  One would indeed think that the results of psycho-analytic studies alone should be sufficient to exclude the volitional criteria, and the unending vagueness of meaning as to personal and impersonal should be sufficient to exclude the personal criteria; but lacking a coherent vision of social activity, such seems not to be the case. External as these criteria are to the definition and classification of social facts, for the purposes of such definition and classification they nevertheless continue to intrude for satisfactions they render those who use them, which satisfactions, again by the showing of results are external to the real problem at issue.

Apparently no progress is made in thought systems that use psychological factors as if known and understood, that hold society and man apart on one side and mind and matter on another, that worry themselves ceaselessly with the question as to just what degree of reality society has anyway, considering the visible presence of so many men. Great progress is being made in assembling materials. Little progress, except in anthropology, is being made in classifying them. The common denominator is missing, the common terms in which the facts can be stated coherently.

§ 68.  *Pedagogical Sociologies.*  There is of course a very considerable organization of social facts into systematic sociologies, but these are almost all made for pedagogical purposes. The pedagogical purpose, entirely legitimate in its place, is however, not the scientific. And it gains no better standing when it presents itself in advance of the latter and assumes its garment. Before the instructor is a great mass of material about man and about society, a certain number of students to whom that material will be very useful and to whom knowledge of it has indeed become essential, and a certain university attitude, differing somewhat in different institutions as to the way young men and young women shall be fitted for life in society. The students come with certain adaptations given them in other branches of study, physics, biology and psychology. They come equipped with the terminologies and habits of understanding used by those other sciences, as well as with the mass of formulated phrasings about man and society in use in everyday life. Instruction in this new field must be given them in accordance with their adaptation. If the instructor cannot formulate his material in those phrasings he has no possibility of function. And this condition will continue until study of sociology systematizes itself from a unified viewpoint as to its material entirely within its own field. After that the translation of its own results into terms of the current bifurcations, such as conscious-unconscious, man-society, actor-environment can be made for pedagogical purposes with definite understanding as to what is being done.

We have here a special case of the use of "frames of reference," something which only the technical investigator needed to take into account before, but which now since the reorganization of physics, every person in touch with scientific development must appreciate. It is a case of the relativity of frames of reference. The usual frames for social facts taken over from psychology or from current living, must be understood as relative and valued only for their approximate uses. The frame that takes in all social facts, in terms of each other, must be kept in mind in reserve, with its own relativity remembered always, despite its wider possibilities of use. In a pedagogical system we may today find elements, forces, processes, products and principles discussed one after the other, when really the same material is being re-worked under each heading, not on the standards of relation within the study, but by standards for connecting it with exterior viewpoints. Unity of vision is lacking no matter how interesting, and how valuable in their particular purpose, the deliveries may be.

# XXII

## Dominance: Clots: Survivals

§ 69. *Dominance: the Power Aspect of Representativeness.* To the little group of definitions we have used, which have specified in Man-society, the Social Fact, as Activity, under its Cross Sectional and Representative characteristics, we might perhaps have added another, that of Dominance. The plan of this essay is however not to specify as far as possible, but to hold back from specification as much as possible, in order better to get the feel of the process. And therefore of dominance and the few other topics remaining to discuss, we shall do nothing more than examine the approach to them.

By dominance, in a setting of representative activities, it will be at once evident that nothing more can be meant than the power aspect of representation; the control value of one activity or set of activities, as selected for description, with reference to another activity or set of activities. And it should be equally evident that no particular type of dominance has any peculiar prerogative over any other in man-society, no matter how spectacular it may be, no matter how we are accustomed to centering on it our attention, no matter what claims it makes for itself or ever has made. The absolute monarch's absoluteness stops flatly in his description of himself and in theories centering around his description, and beyond that it is entirely a matter of representativeness to be analyzed.

§ 70. *Dominance as Two-Directioned.* Dominance is not merely one-directioned, but double-directioned. It is not merely government that dominates underlying activities but underlying activities that dominate government. It is not merely opinions that dominate underlying activities but underlying activities that dominate opinions. The values and meanings must be worked out in both ways before they can hope to be understood in either. The power of ideas must be worked out in terms of the powers that give meaning to those ideas before a measure of the power can be secured. The power of government must be worked out in terms of the powers that express themselves in it before anything more than a superficial estimate of the extent of that power is arrived at. We know this very well at this point or that. We are all of us accustomed to using it from time to time in accordance with our immediate purposes, knowledges and frankness of statement. By a "realist" in politics we mean one who not only works this way but does it systematically and with no camouflage or other pretense. The consideration here is not that something of that kind can be picked out occasionally, if we want to, but that there is no other interpretation possible of the man-society process, in any of its aspects. Essentially the whole process is "realist," no matter what concealments or stoppages of description involve it.

§ 71.  *Interest Groups and Dominance.*  The term "interest groups" deriving from Ratzenhofer, has been referred to as used in earlier studies. It may or may not be a desirable term. That depends on what terminologies we can develop to describe the activities in their connection with one another, without implication of extraneous influences. The interest groups indicate energies taken as direct, at some particular stage of description: taken that is as the pressures which control representative structures, these in turn getting their direct interest statement in addition to their representative statement in varying degrees at varying times. A study in terms of interest groups will be in its first stages complementary to older types of study. Widened and thoroughly stated under exact descriptive terminology for all the activities it will contain the whole process.

§ 72.  *Clotted Dominance.*  Man-society is not a fluid process, its activities freely functioning, each for itself, out to a tenuous gaseous analogy.  The activities cohere, they are clotted.  From the general consideration of dominance we must pass to clotted dominance.  Why use a term like clot instead of talking directly of a type of business organization, a form of government, a polite society group, a philosophy of laissez-faire or of socialism, a great religious system?  Just in order to get away from any pretense to uniqueness in any one of these structures or systems.  Just to get down to what is common to them along with some cooperative habit, some style of hair or dress, some damnation of the momentary national villain or laudation of the momentary hero.

The activities are there but they cohere for expression in this party or that law, in this opinion or that belief, transitory or long-lasting.  They are there and at work as much as the behavior determinations described by psycho-analysts in their complexes.  They are capable of measurement in their cohesions, separations and reorganizations.

Take the feeding activities in an intricate nation

like our own.   We find these built up into very complicated business forms.   We find these business
forms for approximate descriptive purposes, the
same as business forms representing other cross-
sectional activities, not listed as feeding activities,
say clothing, or anything from that to movie-enter-
taining.   We find all these business forms coher-
ing in their representative functions and organizing
and speaking for themselves in a business group with
common denominator terms like rent, wages, interest and profit.   Continuing we find them represented
in governmental and further opinionative activities.
But when the clots are described, as such, no matter how much we may convey in their description,
we have only the beginning for analysis.

Take the political parties as we have them in the
United States today.   Whether in clotted opinionative phases—platform planks—or clotted organization forms, all those questions which everyone has in
mind: whether there is any real difference between
Democratic and Republican national organization,
what the prospects of further survival of these two
organizations are, what the meanings of the straight
party voting and the landslides from one presidential
election to another are, what the chances of the
emergence of a third party are,—all these questions
whether in terms of programs or of personal leader-

ship,—are answerable only by interpretation of the activities that are represented. And if we add to them the problems of the organized control of public opinion in the United States we have possibility of answers only in the same terms.

We have no straight lines containing presumably separate points in man-society, but a complicated many-dimensioned reality, or better said, in the language of today, relativity. Not till the clots, whether structural or opinionative, are stated in all their dimensions are they in way of interpretation and understanding.

§ 73. *Survivals, Dominant and Formal.* The interpretation of survivals, whether with emphasis on survival-dominance or on mere skeleton survival follows directly from this.

We have some great system of belief. In its origins we find it connected with preceding systems and their representative values, and with changed activities and its values for them. We analyze it in its development, its further values and meanings of the same nature, and perhaps, if it establishes itself in a great hierarchy, the ramifications of its connections with every activity we can analyze out for study. The time comes when we describe it in some of its aspects as an anachronism, but that description will not suffice. It is present and strong, and that strength must be led back into its representative values of many kinds, before we can say in what sense it is a survival, and in what not.

Or we may have a gesture that was once a pledge of peace and safety, now a mere formal courtesy. A purple cloak may remain a pride, but be not what once it was.  A word once vital remains as but a jest.

What these things, great and small, were once and what they are now, is capable of determination, and always in the same way.  Then and now the values are real, however different.  It is never enough to say: This idea has become meaningless: that has become hurtful.  We must find the meaning that is left, the hurtfulness or advantages, all in terms of what is hidden beneath.

# XXIII

## Friction: Revolution

§ 74. *Friction.* Despite the extended discussion of recent physics in this text there has been at no time any progress by analogy from physics to sociology. The statement of social facts in their own terms has been won by several generations of investigators in their own field, and by the more recent theorists whose work has been described in a preceding chapter. At this point however an illustration may be used, which, though frequently enough used before, is so apt as to be worth while for shortening the statement. It is between friction and explosion in physics and friction and revolution in society.

In each case we have sets of actions diverted from their described trends into wastes and heat. Frictions in each case are called such only by the test of what is outlined for and expected of the action. Explosions have indeed in physics been brought under control and forced to do a desired work. And against that, revolutions have their curative value when all else fails.

Friction in society involves the appearance of representative activities specialized under a new description of phenomena, and appearing under the old descriptions as a retardation of activities of the latter. These representative activities may use any social technique; any form of violence, blows, imprisonments, killings, spasmodic or in regulated systems; any form of trickery, spasmodic or organized; any form of argument, spasmodic or organized.

§ 75. *Revolution.* When the frictions and retardations reach a certain degree the result is explosive action, revolution. This again appears as either destructive or recuperative, according to what cross-sectional judgment is applied. So deadly serious becomes the reaction that no sense of consistency or humor, in terms of individual psychology, may mitigate it. The same man on the same day in the same speech may laud revolution to the skies when he is talking of 1776, making it of absolute worth: and he may damn it in equally absolute terms as the destruction of all human values, when he is talking of 1924. That the reverse judgments have been made or are being made in other opinionative representative fields, is however evident. A lightning bolt may either be regarded as destructive from the point of view of the activities containing the building hit, or recuperative from those wider activities involving general atmospheric conditions. The explosion of a mine on a battle line is destructive from the position of the defenders, path-clearing from the position of the attackers.

§ 76. *Opinion and Revolution.* To interpret a revolution in terms of opinions without investigating their representative values, or to interpret it in terms of governmental forms without investigating their representative values in actual man-society terms, is simply to assume all our answers in advance. Such interpretations set up actors, personify them, externalize and degrade the environmental characteristics, and ignore the fact that what is thrown out as environment is really vital to the full description of what is retained as actor. They are entirely justified in their capacity of representative activities themselves. All that they need is further specification in such a way that their place in the whole process is shown. Widen them in the way here proposed and they are still representative activities, but with this difference that they take up the others within themselves, apply much more fully, and tend to reach the limits of what at this time appears as practicable with the scientific social field.

§ 77. *Swift and Slow Revolution.* As in explosions, so in revolutions, we have accumulations and specifications of activity, temporary statuses, pauses in the more coarsely observed phenomena, and then the disruptive phenomena and attendant rearrangements of action. What happens to this man or that man, this institution or that institution, is not the whole story. Nor does the whole story lie in what happens to all of the men involved taken as individuals, nor to all the institutions involved, taken as determinate. It is as superficial as the description of a mine explosion merely in terms of the earth displaced, the smoke and vapors, and the disappearance of the explosive. Behind such facts lies for the explosion a complex chemical statement, and for the revolution a complex social statement.

Slow revolutions are differentiated from violent revolutions in technique, not in underlying forces. The techniques themselves are representative activities. Which kind of revolution comes may be stated in terms of the plasticity of the society, but that again has no statement except in terms of full analysis of cross sectional activities in their varying energies and forms of representativeness.

## XXIV

## Progress

§ 78. *Not Progress.* It is hard for sociology to get along without a theory of progress—but necessary. Every theory of progress requires some standard or set of standards, some scale of measurement. That scale must either come from without or from within. If it comes from without it is irrelevant. If it comes from within, then every statement of progress must be absorbed in Relativity.

It is true, of course, that the standard coming from without does not really come from without. It only presents itself as if it did. It lays claim to an external authority, and pretends to an absoluteness, which is under analysis a matter of verbiage. Every theory of progress is under an obligation to examine not merely the values, but the sources and meanings of its standards. Every such examination will lead back into activities of man-society for those sources and meanings. When so led back the

positive generalized theory of progress disappears.
It is only by stopping part way, by refusing to go
back to evident meanings, that Progress as such can
be discussed.

§ 79. *But Progresses.* Not progress, but progresses, is what we find in man-society. In an expanding activity a progress can be measured in
extent of territory, duration of time, number of heads
counted. In the politics of elections it can be measured by votes: in business it can be measured by
dollars either of turnover or of profit: For one purpose a progress can be measured by divorce statistics, for another by police court records, for another
by the extension of the control of nature, for another
by suicides. And so it goes. But for each such
statement, the exact social activity must be specified
in terms of which the valuation is made.

The examination of progress is not different from
the examination of process. There is only a little
difference in the emphasis of statement. In each
case we have relativity, the statement of one described activity in terms of others. With process
we talk of it in terms of meaning, of interpretation.
With progress we talk of it in terms of values. But
always the question is: Values—for what?

Generalize as far as you will. Say that "through
the ages one increasing purpose runs." Down you

come, if you do not deliberately close your eyes and stop your work at some point in the analysis to a description of the increase and of the purpose in terms of the activities of man-society. And the very eye-closing and work-stopping is part of that activity. What it is actually representative of others will point out, if not you.

§ 80. *Typical Current Standards.* Can we say that the progressive elimination of pain is progress? Yes,—in special cases, along special lines of limited duration, as for instance in the use of anæsthetics, or in the rules of war. No, when we take longer duration of human history, and run back further into biological history. Construct society with pain eliminated during the course of the next thousand years—you cannot conceive today what you would have. Pain is this evil or that evil—but evil generally with progress absolutely in its elimination? It would be rash perhaps to say No, but vastly rasher to say Yes. An earthquake is a pain-bringer on a great scale. We would hail as a progress scientific efforts for the avoidance of its effects. But an earth without earthquakes? Scientists tell us all life would disappear.

Do we make man the standard of values and test progress by him? Man in that sense is an arbitrary construction, a clotting of meanings, the outcome of a bifurcation, based not on knowledge but on very limited examination. Into that clot, the individual man, or man generalized, must be read its interpretation in activities of Man-Society, all relative. Do we run a series, as is so common, of progress from instincts through custom to rational procedure in society? It is frankly a laughable series, its little peep-hole at society readily located and described.

§ 81. *The Most Coherent Progress, that of Science, is Itself the Bearer of Relativity.* We can come nearer to progress in general by examining scientific progress than in any other way. Here we have working knowledge, working ever more fully, and tending ever to wider agreement in statement and in use among all the workers. We seem to be constructing a coherent world at last. But, alas, it is just here that Relativity is most vivid, no longer as the proof, but as the structure of the progress itself.

We come to this. We may use the term progress as much as we wish. But we must take it in durations, and as well in extensions and energies. When we have established our series of terms in this way, we may stop if we wish, but thereby we clot ourselves in the process at that point. And our very clotting must be interpreted either by ourselves or by some other investigators. We are back again in the relativities of Man-Society.

# XXV

## World Peace: Socio-Analysis

§ 82. *Racial Arrogance.* Views of progress are knitted with opinions of superiority. They are not merely the constructions of dreamers and theorists: they rest in a background of opinion used continuously in all every-day living. The opinions of superiority represent assertively our going process of existence. And they represent it, as every investigator knows all too well, in a terminology of ignorance. Their dominance and appearances of dominance can be traced back representatively through other activities. They are clots outstanding in many respects among all other clots of Man-Society. Not merely the superiorities of individuals or small groups or classes, but those of nations or races are full of violence.

§ 83. *A Position Against War.* Let us take a position frankly identifying ourselves with certain activities of society, identifying ourselves, if we care to put it that way with certain interests in society. Let this position be against war, not war absolutely or war forever, but war in the next generation or the next century between the nations as they now exist. We need not worry, against some one's argument, out of what frying pan into what fire we may fall if we succeed in our project, if we put a check to wars. We answer we will meet those new perils when we come to them, and we have no fear that our desires and energies and struggles will disappear all too soon under folded angels' wings if we win out. We point to the new powers of destruction, the cheapened cost of destruction, the widened range of destruction, the threat to the old men and the women and children in the homes as well as to the soldiers in the field, the wastes and after-burdens, the possible weakening of all "our" civilization against other civilizations, or against fertile and as yet uncivilized forces of potential mastery. We know that there are profits in wars to certain activities of our own, but we say they are profits of short durations, and we say that in longer durations those apparent profits are losses, and the real profits will come on our side of the argument. We clot ourselves, but we know we are doing it.

§ 84. *Obscurantism.* What now is the procedure? We are all of us involved, as it is, in this ques-

tion in the fields of opinion.   But the opinion, all of
it, no matter what length of argument it may follow, what mass of detail facts it may examine, tends
to run down into expression of old absolute words,
not of relativities.   The conclusions come out in
the form of "is" and "should be" and "must be"
not in weighted statements of the energies and meanings of each part of the process.   "Is" and "must"
are the great tools of obscurantism.   "Is" and
"must" with sneer and jeer and arrogant assertion
are the backbone of propaganda, and they hide the
weighted value of what is behind the propaganda.
They give us great organized procedures in our own
age of "enlightenment" today not at all inappro-
priate for comparison with what, when we look back
to the Middle Ages we call their worst aspect.

§ 85.   *Socio-Analysis*.   The answer, almost the
sole hope, is in bringing out fully and continuously
and systematically, the meanings and value and
weights of all the opinionative phases in terms of all
the activities that are at play.   It is a process of
socio-analysis that we need, not unworthy perhaps
of being contrasted in that phrase with the work of
psycho-analysis.   The hidden things can come into
the light, and the light will be curative.   Everywhere around us parts of our social activity are cast-
ing their demands absolutely against the social

sky, ignoring their relativity, stating themselves in language-thought structures which split themselves off from their origin in activity and attempt to justify that from which they arise. Clear statements must replace them giving the meanings of words and thoughts, slogans and ideals, policies and doctrines in terms of their groupal origins and groupal bearers.

Then the conflicts which are now obscure and concealed, not unlike the analysts' inhibitions in the unconscious he studies, will come up into full view, ready for resolution into something of peace and harmony of living and effectiveness of action.

§ 86. *Education.* Little can be done until our knowledge is recast into explicit terms of activities, and not much perhaps until a greater extension is secured of what knowledge we now have. Education is the word we now use to indicate the process of influencing society in its more respectable forms, but education has two great aspects, one as it fits the individual for effective action in some certain groupal complex, the other as it loosens him from some of his special attachments and widens him for other and more profitable attachments. But all too little of our education goes beyond fitting for the more profitable in one of the narrowest usages of that word. Even our universities with the broadest cultural claims often stop that culture, even restrict it and hamper it, before it gives comprehension of the real groupal aspects of the coming young man's and young woman's life. Even our churches too often harden men and women in their positions in society and satisfy them therewith, instead of freeing them to comprehension of their own position's value in terms of all the positions around them.

§ 87. *Sympathy.* Sympathy is the term from the life of feeling which is concurrent with the education of the understanding of society, in which we see hope to break down its conflicts. Sympathy may lead far. Education in sympathy is however not to be attained by direct attack so as to produce it and make it produce in turn the results the world craves. It has been tried too often. Knowledge of meanings must be the hard path we follow.

§ 88. *The Resolvability of Frictions.* There is no magic power. There is no leap over great social distances. The distance from group to group is measurable by resistance. The resistance may be overcome by the sledge: it sinks in: it is under cover: it recurs. It may be overcome by small stages of advance in understanding. A patriotism that is over-wrought till it carries the seeds of death will not be overcome by anti-patriotism, nor will that in turn be overcome by anti-anti-patriotism. A patiotism that is enlightened and carries seeds of life will be furthered by analysis and interpretation of the many varied elements that enter into the great complex that is the nation. The forces and energies and pressures are present in the activities: It is a question of the technique with which they work themselves out. It is step by step.

We have no right to say that human nature compels our conflicts, from those of families and local societies and communities up to those of nations. It is human nature working with bad tools.

Because we stand at a time of great conflicts we have no right to say those conflicts are irresolvable. All social life is a resolution of conflicts, provisional always, with new conflicts arising, with the intolerable activities being driven out, with new methods being secured, with destructions at times and places, but with new creations succeeding.

Knowledge of our group attachments and their relativities—that, and that alone, can give us the greater approximations to virile peace which is what we all most crave, and of what we all most despair in the hidden parts of our lives, while our values are given us in darkness.

# XXVI

## The Argument Inspected

§ 89. *Problem.* Seeking an exact statement of facts in the Man-Society field with a view to coherent interpretation in a functioning system what is the best point of approach in the light of the present status of physics, psychology and sociology?

§ 90. *Material.* We possess great masses of information, accumulated for the most part by the investigations of the last fifty years, partially examined and arranged for better understanding. Development has been towards an ever more complete statement of this material as directly and immediately social, and towards the exclusion of extraneous interpretative factors. Such extraneous factors still persist, however, in all systems, either:

(*a*) in the form of reference to absolutes or the bastard offspring of absolutes, such as the personified society, the social whole, absolute or definitely determinable general progress, sovereignty, and social psychologies of various types super-ordinated to individual psychology; or

(*b*) in the form of reference to factors of human nature posited as pre-social or extra-social in such sense that they are given a content sufficiently "outside" of the social to be used to explain the social: such factors as idea, ideals, purposes having been largely abandoned, but such factors as instincts still persisting, though with continually reduced number and definiteness.

This material appears framed under the four bifurcations of matter-mind, conscious-unconscious, man-society and actor-environment, none of them efficient postulates for social investigation except in its preliminary stages.

§ 91. *Scientific Status.* As a system this information lacks observational coherence, because it has no common denominator for the man and the society aspects of the facts: because the extra-social elements brought in as interpretative factors come in terms and in definitions which, no matter how well they may seem to work in their own fields, have never been properly fused for the man-society field: because their various background implications make impossible any common terminological meeting ground for investigators.

§ 92. *The Contribution of Psychology.* Abandonment of an extra-verbal reality of mind and the powers of mind, and of all terms deriving from them: reduction of consciousness and of all related terms from facts postulated as directly known to the position of very obscure problems: an increasingly complete specification of the individual in terms of his behavior: a concentration on psychological process and function instead of on psychic qualities taken concretely: a pending identification of thought process with language process on the basis of minute motor discharges of a language nature in connection with brain processes of a thought nature.

§ 93. *Weakness of Psychology, Not In Its Own Field, But When Taken Over at Its Own Statement into the Study of Man-Society.* As a study of behavior it postulates the organism as separate from its environment, whereas all social facts contain the actor-environment activity in such form that it must be envisaged as a whole, that is to say, must be taken under one unified statement, as one activity: so that, within its behavior, psychology still takes over and keeps very much content which is of the very essence of the man-society problem to be examined: with the result that all interpretations of society in terms of these man psychological factors start by begging the question.

§ 94. *The Contribution of Physics.* The new physics, in its quality of high achievement against which we must test the value of our infant analysis of society, no longer requires us to keep a background of space time and matter around our terms. Matter has become for physics merely a descriptive term indicating one group of its phenomena, which is separated from its other phenomena, not by an understood barrier, but by an open problem, at present located in the connection of the positive electron with the nucleus of the atom. Space and time are relativities within its analysis.

§ 95. *A Joint Contribution of Physics and Psychology.* Physics gives us Action, a unity of energy in time. Psychology gives us Behavior, a specification of activity. The durational-dimensional energies of physics fall into series with the behavior of psychology in such a way that we need have no further bother from any verbal background of matter and mind in studying man-society. The series today is not Matter-Mind but Radiation-Behavior, with a vaguely outlined province of radiation indicated by the word Matter, and a vaguely outlined province of Behavior indicated by the word consciousness.

§ 96. *The Rebellion Against Verbal Tyrannies.* As physics has destroyed the extra-functional implications of the words space and time, and as psychology has destroyed the similar implications of the word consciousness and of all dependent words, and as all our words when not fully functioning with others in the particular system in which they are being used prove to be but impasses to thought: we are at a point where we no longer dare to rely on any terms carried over from one field into another, but must strike them out in each field except as we can make them function freely with other terms in that field, prior to connecting through their revision different fields, as our knowledge proceeds. The world of our study is no longer a world of subjects and predicates.

§ 97. *Weakness of the Old Physical-Psychological Series as Applied Directly to Social Fact*. As a point of limitation, of caution, rather than of positive guidance, we may observe that while physics (barring its present somewhat speculative difficulty with the electronic orbits) appears to build up its world out of elements measurably "smaller," and by usual acceptance in Euclidean space forms, "within" its phenomena under interpretation, man-society in contrast presents its phenomena in a fashion of comprehensiveness, of "oneness" in such sense that every definition it makes must exclude a sharp "otherness," so as to cover or contain not merely the extensions of the phenomena but also their durational anticipations. . . . Implications of "nearness" and "farness" of "inside" and "outside" are among those which must be stripped from the older view of physics and psychology,—and indeed so far as physics is concerned are in way of such stripping at present for its own purpose,—before the status of social facts in these aspects comes clear.

§ 98. *Relativities in Present Sociology.* Compared with the dogmatisms of a few generations ago, and with the dogmatisms of men practically active in specialized and localized phases of social life today, careful students of society have become very cautious in their assertions, both as to realities and as to values. Not only are they ceasing to state and to judge all other societies by the one they have in the forefront of their knowledge. They are coming to recognize that every judgment they make reflects the appearance of other phases of society from some one phase or system of phases at which they place themselves, and has no basis for any confidence of statement, other than in terms of the particular social phase in which its statement rests. Generalize this development. Let the tests of every phase of society be in terms of some other phase or phases. Formulate statements that always specify this dependence.  Formulate them in such a way that exact meanings can be conveyed from one investigator to another, thereby gaining the beginnings of measurement.  Assemble these statements and judgments carrying their relative references with them under typical forms.  Then the study of man-society acquires a real relativity not unworthy to be brought within the lines of physical relativity.  Then a science has arrived.

§ 99.  *Time and Space in Social Facts.*  Social facts as we can specify them today are not required to take any of the local times and spaces of physics, but they may in accordance with the province of their own examination present themselves in their own dimensions and durations, assimilable to the relativity of durations and dimensions in physics. Durations the investigator may choose freely as is expedient at each stage.  Distances in the old sense of dead intervals of space are no bar to treating as one fact what occurs across many individuals who themselves to daily vision are separated in space. Above all the instantaneous, with all its implications of set existence, already barred as it is from physics, is wholly meaningless for man-society.

§ 100.  *Cross-Sectional Activity of Man-Society.* The social fact which we can hold before us to classify and study presents itself as a cross-sectional or groupal activity resting in many man-lives, and nowhere else: not capable of definition in terms of any one life or summation of separate lives: never instantaneously existing but always defined in a period of time: not losing its observational single-ness of fact because the lives in which it rests are, if individually defined, found in separate regions of space: always involving past and future man-society references.

§ 101. *Representativeness of Social Facts.* Each cross-sectional activity in man-society must be so stated as to include in its meaning its full purpos-iveness with reference to other social facts: purpos-iveness being taken merely as a descriptive word pointing at the full network of anticipations, energy-directions and goal-values wherever found, with-out their reference, or the reference of any of them or any phases among them, to loci outside the described activity. Nowhere do we have baldly a social fact in a special determination of space and time and another social fact in some other special determination of space and time, and a relation, causal, or what-not, between them. Such bald statements are at most useful where the material is comparatively unorganized, and go no further than to indicate a possible problem of study. At grips with our study the very definition of each activity involves other activities and is made in terms of representativeness with reference to them, all governmental and opinionative activities of society being capable of being brought fully and with heightened meaning under such definition.

§ 102. *Background Obscurities.* In truth a background of vague understanding remains, but it is far different from the old one, and has lost in large measure its deadening effects. In place of the old bifurcations, we have atmospheric difficulties: physics building "up" and "out," as the words run, towards the inclusion of society; man-society building "down" and "in" towards the inclusion of physics: splittings of observation set over against comprehensiveness of observation: particularizing and unifying aspects with no clean understanding by us of what the words imply or even trend towards implying: along with them attenuated surviving queries as to personality and individuality: persistent "human nature" or more exactly put "physical nature" theories. But no matter how wrong we may be shown to be later under some new statement, we have for the present a working ground towards rightness, a great sweeping away of obstacles.

§ 103. *A Complaint.* Statements of method are of little import compared with results in work. Is this outline worth while? Simply so far as it summarizes the direction in which the study of society has actually been proceeding, clarifies some of the surviving crudities in the explanatory statement of the facts and makes possible more exact and definite formulations of the facts for cooperative use by the workers in the field.

# XXVII

## Hints for Guidance in Study

§ 104. *The Substance of Postulates and Rules.* I might frame the following remarks as postulates or methodological rules. I prefer to present them as hints for guidance in study. No postulate or rule is more than that except as it secures further description and name from the rigor and success of its application.

I. No term, however useful in practical life or in other science, has any forthwith claim to recognition in the study of man-society within which all such terms take their origin.

The bifurcations of matter-mind and of conscious-unconscious have at most a preliminary descriptive value.

The bifurcation of man-society, when postulated, begs all interpretative questions in advance.

The bifurcation of actor-environment breaks down anew with each step in interpretative advance.

II. No terms may be used which are not commensurable, involving a common denominator of meaning.

III. No social fact may be taken except as a cross-section of a number of human lives, over which the Euclidean space form has no determining control.

IV. No social fact is ever instantaneously present, but always in durations, involving pasts and futures, and involving by this same token full anticipatory and purposive values.

V. No social fact may be taken in terms of its own description of itself, but every social fact must be taken in terms of its representative values for all other social facts, or so many of these as can be brought into play without present powers of determination.

VI. No value reference may be universalized for an assumed social whole.

VII. No posited individual man, nor any abstraction or personification of him may be used as a measure or standard of value.

§ 105. *Cautions.* The following remarks, more casual in nature may be added:

The first duty of each one of us in investigating is to analyze and bring out clearly to ourselves the social cross-sectional activities we ourselves are identified with and representing, not only generally, but in each special piece of work.

What we are used to is bad guide in examining what we are not used to.

What is emphasized around us is no test of what is scientifically important around us.

What is emphasized around us is no test either of what is emphasized or scientifically important in societies socially remote from us: and social remoteness may coexist with nearness in time and in Euclidean space.

Our commonest error is to fall back in one way or another upon human nature, and when we do it we may always know that we are concealing ignorance by duplicating statement.

§ 106. *The Future of Relativity.* The partial social relativity we have gradually gained in experience and in studying widens into a complete social relativity, meeting physical relativity without conflict and with fair hopes of cooperative advance.

# COMMENT AND REFERENCE

# PART I

## The Meaning of Relativity

The discussion of the meaning of Einstein and of Relativity in Part I binds together throughout several different chains of materials:

The admitted practical everyday relativity of views among men.

The new physical relativity.

The social setting of the new physical relativity.

The crushing critique of language given by this new physical relativity.

The foundations laid in it for a wider social relativity.

These may all be said to find their unity in the new language-thought attitude of scientific workers covering both physics and society, a field in which I have no contribution to make, but which I present simply as involving limitations much less troublesome to scientific advance than those of the last generation.

I am not aware of drawing anything from physics or any other science for use in the statement or interpretation of social facts, either by deduction or analogy. The nearest that I come to using even an analogy is in a detail in Chapter XXIII.

The discussion of the new physics is necessary solely to show that the scientific background it gives us is no longer inharmonious with what our direct examination of man and of society reports to us. While this new physics centers entirely in Einstein, the underlying meanings are much more fully developed by men like Whitehead and Eddington, and Schlick and Weyl. Whether their attitude is critical or not towards Einstein's technical results in part or whole, they are a unit in the acceptance of the new cosmos which Einstein has revealed. Criticisms of Einstein based on the word meanings of the old physics are simply negligible. They are as antiquated and valueless as alchemy.

### I. Man, Society and Einstein

P. 3. Albert Einstein was born in Ulm, Germany, in 1879. He studied at Zürich University intending to become a teacher. Instead he spent seven years, 1902–9, as engineer in the Swiss patent office. He became connected with the

Zürich faculty in 1909, went to Prague as a professor in 1911, and returned to Zürich as professor in the following year. In 1914 he was called to the Prussian Academy of Science at Berlin, and was given a professorship at Berlin University, and became also a director of the Institute for Physical Research. His paper "On the Electro-Dynamics of Moving Bodies," 1905, announced his first principle of relativity, and his paper "The Foundations of the Generalized Theory of Relativity," in 1916, gave the full extension to gravitation. His most important achievements are listed by H. L. Brose, *The Theory of Relativity*, biographical note, as

1905  The Special Theory of Relativity.
   The discovery that all forms of energy possess inertia.
   The laws underlying the Brownian movement.
   The quantum law of the emission and absorption of light.
1907  The fundamental notions of the general theory of relativity.
1912  The recognition of the non-Euclidean nature of space-determination and its connection with gravitation.
1915  Gravitational field equations.
   Explanation of the motion of Mercury's perihelion.

To become acquainted with Einstein the non-technical reader will probably have to hunt through the discussions till he finds the work best suited by its particular manner of approach for his needs. The Einstein film is very useful where it can be seen, and Garrett P. Serviss' little picture book based upon the film, "The Einstein Theory of Relativity" is helpful by way of displaying the paradoxes in a vivid way. H. Dingle's short book *Relativity for All* is one of the best. Eddington's essay in the *Scientific Monthly*, January, 1923, and Birkhoff's in the same periodical March, 1924, are especially good. On a larger scale are Charles Nordmann's *Einstein and the Universe*, Eddington's *Space, Time and Gravitation*, and Moritz Schlick's *Space and Time in Contemporary Physics*. Einstein's own popular treatise *Relativity, the Special and the General Theory* is one of the best. On a more technical investigation, Whitehead's *The Principle of Relativity*, and Eddington's *The Mathematical Theory of Relativity* are important.

## II.  The Term "Einstein"—Its Meanings

P. 6. "Some of which . . . have *made* the whole fraternity . . . whirl." Notice this word "made" and consider the difficulties of statement.

The point of the argument, not only in this chapter but throughout this book is that such a use of subject, predicate and object give most imperfect description for which better can and must be substituted.

And yet, if I attempt at the outset to use what I know to be more exact description, I shall appear diffuse and vague, losing emphasis on the very fact I wish here to indicate. Hence I retain here the apparently vigorous expression of current speech, point out in this note that it is a poor approximation to exact description, and that its appearance of vigor is a delusion, and leave it to the developing argument to interpret it.

And why this violation in phrasing of my own meaning? Because it is in this essay, not a question of exact technical description of social facts, but of explaining, justifying and interpreting in terms of common intercourse such exact technical description about the same subject matter. Exact technical description may be made as between students who have a common meeting ground in the attitude of this essay, or of some modification of it, or of some substitute for it. And between them it will be clear and simple. But to start out with it in this place would make most difficult reading for people whose frame of statement is not merely the common meanings of subject, predicate and object, but all the background of obscurity and evasion which they contain. If I held steadily to it in this essay, I would almost destroy the possibility for any such reader of following the argument.

Many a word can be picked out in what I write for criticism from my own point of view. I shall welcome the criticism if made justly as an imperfect conveyance of fact. I take this occasion, however, to reject all such criticism and deny its validity if made to indicate my own departure from my own argument. A definite understanding on this point will help matters from the beginning.

P. 7. The phrase "the physical world" may not be taken as meaning anything more than the world physically stated.

P. 8. On the experimental verification of Einstein's calculations, see Eddington's *Space, Time and Gravitation*, Chapters VII and VIII. Also appendix III to Einstein's *Relativity, the Special and the General Theory*. Investigations of the wave lengths of the solar spectrum with reference to the predicted Einstein displacement have been made by St. John at Mt. Wilson Observatory, and by Director Curtis and Dr. Burns and Dr. Meggers, the last named of the Bureau of Standards, at the Allegheny Observatory. Both show in addition to what is known as "the limb effect" a curious progressive shift, which ranges from less than the Einstein prediction for very faint solar lines, to more for very strong lines, the range being from about one quarter of the Einstein prediction to about double. At Allegheny University the results are considered a negation of the Einstein prediction. (See *Science*, May 16, 1924). St. John on the other hand believes that he can account for most, but not all, of this progressive shift in full accord with the Einstein prediction. All that can now be said, therefore, is that there are complications of such nature that no definite decision can yet be made. A recent report on experiments testing Einstein predictions is made by Prof. Henry Norris Russell in *Scientific American*, Aug. 19, 1925, covering Michelson and Gale's work in 1924, Prof. D. C. Miller's work, and the observations on the faint companion star of Sirius. Prof. Russell heads his article "Remarkable New Tests Favor the Einstein Theory." See Afterword of the present book.

P. 9. Gauss had devised a method of studying a surface in Euclidean space without using the Cartesian coordinates, or attributing to it any of the assumed qualities of Euclidean space. "Gauss indicated the principles according to which we can treat the geometrical relationships in the surface and thus pointed out the way to the method of

Riemann of treating multi-dimensional non-Euclidean continua." (Einstein, *Relativity, the Special and the General Theory* Chapter XXIV). Gauss' work formed the starting point for all the new geometries.

Euclid's axiom was that through a given point, only one straight line parallel to a given line can be drawn. No one ever succeeded in proving it. Hence the alternative axioms were tried.

Lobatchewsky's axiom was that through a given point many straight lines parallel to a given line can be drawn, and he built a geometry upon it. The younger Bolyai independently developed a similar geometry.

Riemann's axiom was that through a given point no straight line parallel to a given line can be drawn, and he built his geometry upon that. It was found later that Riemann's geometry contained the geometry of a spherical surface as a particular case within it. See Poincaré's *Science and Hypothesis*, p. 37.

For these geometries reference may be made to Steinmetz's *Four Lectures on Relativity and Space*, p. 72 and following.

P. 10. Euclid's geometry has also been extended into many dimensions, but Eddington states that it would take ten dimensions in Euclid to make the computations that with Riemann are made in four. *Space, Time and Gravitation*, p. 84.

P. 10. The treatment of light under relativity is well put by William Pepperrell Montague in an article critical towards relativity in the *Philosophical Review*, vol. 33, p. 146: "All events on any one light ray happen at the same point instant in the space time of the world." Light therefore appears like zero in that it apparently stands still, while on the other hand it is like infinity in that it is not at all altered by additions or subtractions.

When for the first time a non-technical reader endeavors to get hold of relativity he is apt to be puzzled by the prominence given the fixed speed of light, for this seems to do violence to the very relativity which is built upon it as a postulate. The affair appears better to him, however, when he finds that it is not the velocity of light concretely taken that is in question, but that it is a limiting velocity, a highest velocity known, to which light approximates, that is involved. Whitehead, *The Principle of Relativity*, p. 9, puts it this way, that "the symmetrical properties of relative velocity issue in a critical velocity 'c' which is defined without reference to the velocity of light." Criticism of relativity on account of this specially favored position of light fails, therefore, first because the special position of light is a deliberately chosen postulate, secondly because the unique action of light is the experimental starting point for the whole theory, and thirdly because it proves not to be the light wave concretely that holds a unique position, but instead that the velocity of light just happens observationally to be very close to a limit within which relativity operates. What appears like a point for criticism at the start therefore develops into a phase of the whole background of the theory of relativity, which is a maze of units and limits and periodical relations. See Chapter VII.

P. 12. For Minkowski's work on time, see Chapter VI, p. 48. D'Alembert in 1754 had suggested that time might be regarded as fourth dimension, though it was for him only an interesting observation, which he did not like to father himself, and so attributed to an unnamed friend.

P. 13. Of his general theory, Einstein says in beginning his *The Foundation of the General Theory of Relativity* (translation Saha and Bose): "The generalization of the relativity theory has been made much easier through the form given to the special relativity theory by Minkowski, which mathematician was the first to recognize clearly the formal equivalence of the space-like and time-like coordinates, and who made use of it in the building up of the theory. The mathematical apparatus used for the general relativity theory lay already complete in the Absolute Differential Calculus, which were based on the researches of Gauss, Riemann and Christoffel on the non-Euclidean manifold, and which have been shaped into a system by Ricci and Levi-civita, and already applied to the problems of theoretical physics. I thank my friend Grossmann, by whose help I was not only spared the study of the mathematical literature pertinent to this subject, but who also aided me in the researches on the field equations of gravitation."

P. 13.   Physics, of course, does not concern itself with the life of the observer, in its calculations, in any other respect than his velocity, in reference to which other velocities are observed and measured by him.

P. 13.

| Gauss | 1777–1855 | critical publication | 1827 |
|---|---|---|---|
| Lobatchewsky | 1793–1856 | " " | 1826–1840 |
| Bolyai | 1802–1860 | " " | 1842 |
| Riemann | 1826–1866 | " " | 1854 |
| Michelson | 1852 | " " | 1887 |
| Fitzgerald | 1851–1901 | " " | 1891–3 |
| Lorentz | 1853 | " " | 1893–5 |
| Minkowski | 1864–1909 | " " | 1908 |

P. 14.   For justification of what is called the social statement of Einstein's work, reference must be made to Part III.   The common statement assumes that the unit man, Einstein, did so and so, and that definite detached causes operated upon him from the work of other unit men.   I have no quarrel with this ordinary statement in terms of a causal punching of one man by another, so far as its ordinary uses go. The point here is merely that the thought-activity statement is truer than the individual man statement, and that it is the former statement to which attention must be directed.

"Einstein" in all pertinent discussions becomes not a man, but a label of many varying significances. The moment one is beyond the technical field of an exact comparison of his calculations with the calculations of some other worker, then, even for physicists, much more is referred to than a certain German. It is hardly conceivable even in loose language and loose analysis that if Einstein had lived a hundred years ago, before the contributors to his thought system had done their work, he could have got his present results. Had he secured them they would have failed in confirmation and been shelved. Had he insisted too much on them, he would have been popularly regarded not as a genius but as insane. He might even have been visited with one of the many forms of social punishment which range from burning at the stake, or confinement in an asylum, to slow death from poverty and contempt.

### III. Relativity in Physics

P. 17. The term relativity, so far as I am aware, prior to Einstein, was not as much used in English as in French or German. In French the phrase was "principle of relative motion," and in German "principle of relativity." (See G. Moch, *La Relativité des Phénomènes*, Introduction.) Einstein used the phrase current in his language, calling his first treatment, the special theory of relativity and his later treatment, the general theory.

In contrast with Einstein's theory the earlier relativity, now referred to as mechanical relativity, Galilean relativity or Newtonian relativity is contained in Newton's fifth corollary to his laws of motion as follows: "The motions of bodies included in a given space are the same amongst themselves, whether that space is at rest, or moves uniformly forwards in a right line without any circular motion." (Motte translation.) Leaving out the problems of rotational motion, this comes to saying that mechanical motions in any given system are all relative to one another, as we know them, and that no absolute motion can be detected. The specialist puts it thus: "The laws of mechanics remain unchanged in form for any transformation from one set of inertial axes to another" (Brose, *The Theory of Relativity*, p. 10), or thus: "It is impossible by means of any dynamical phenomena to ascertain absolutely the velocity of any material particle, but the relative velocity of any point with respect to any other is a uniquely determinable quantity" (Cunningham, *The Principle of Relativity*, p. 4).

Einstein's special theory of relativity proceeded on the basis of the limiting velocity of light, accepting this and giving new foundations to Newtonian relativity so far as it had been apparently undermined by the crudities of ether theories. At this stage he retained Euclidean space and Galilean coordinates, but substituted Lorentzian transformations for Galilean. His special theory applies to uniform motions.

His general theory applies to all motions, not only uniform but difform or accelerated. Gravitation becomes the principal special case. Accepting Minkowski's interpretation of time, and substituting the use of Gaussian coordinates for Cartesian, he secured equations invariant for all transformations. He puts it thus: "All Gaussian coordinate systems are essentially equivalent for the formulation of the general laws of nature." And again: "According to the general theory of relativity by application of arbitrary substitutions of the Gauss variables, the equations must pass over into equations of the same form: for every transformation (not only the Lorentz transformation) corresponds to the transition of one Gauss coordinate system into another" (*Relativity, the Special and the General Theory*, Chap. XXVIII). This is put by Bolton, *An Introduction to the Theory of Relativity*, as follows: "Relativity as a whole is the theory of the statement of general physical laws in forms common to all observers" (p. vi.).

The following statement made by Einstein to a correspondent of the New York *Times* seems worth quoting in full:

"The term relativity refers to time and space. According to Galileo and Newton, time and space were absolute entities, and the moving systems of the universe were dependent on the absolute time and space. On this conception was built the science of mechanics. The resulting formulas sufficed for all motions of a slow nature: it was found, however, that they would not conform to the rapid motions apparent in electro-dynamics.

"This led the Dutch professor Lorentz and myself to develop the theory of special relativity. Briefly it discards absolute time and space and makes them in every instance relative to moving systems. By this theory all phenomena in electro-dynamics, as well as in mechanics, hitherto irreducible by the old formulas—and there are multitudes—were satisfactorily explained.

"Till now it was believed that time and space

existed by themselves, even if there was nothing else—no sun, no stars, no earth—while now we know that time and space are not the vessel for the universe, but could not exist at all if there were no contents, namely no sun, earth and other celestial bodies.

"This special relativity, forming the first part of my theory, relates to all systems moving with uniform motion: that is, moving in a straight line with equal velocity.

"Gradually I was led to the idea seeming a very paradox in science that it might apply equally to all moving systems, even of difform motion, and thus I developed the conception of general relativity which forms the second part of my theory." (Quoted in the introduction to *The Einstein Theory of Relativity*, by Prof. H. A. Lorentz.)

P. 19.  An interesting variation of early ideas of space is found among Pueblo Indians, and in some other American and Australian tribes, among whom space is regarded as circular and divided into as many regions as there are clans or groups of clans in the tribe, each clan with its nomenclature and symbols appertaining to a particular region of the space.  See almost any volume of American anthropology, or Durkheim, *The Elementary Forms of the Religious Life*, p. 12.

P. 21. With the word Ether, as well as with matter and with space and time in the Newtonian sense, we observe how physics has always insisted on carrying itself in a background of common word meanings. The physicists for the most part, no matter how free they have kept themselves from the use of these words in their calculations, have had no sense of satisfaction without them, until Einstein came to give them release. So far as an outsider to the science may be permitted to judge almost the entire list of critics of Einstein is composed of men who are controlled by a sentimental attachment to a word which they can't give up— men who are, so to speak, lodged in their ether, and can't get beyond it.

Einstein himself seems peculiarly uninterested in the fate of such terms, and it must be noted that he does not go so far as most of his followers go in excluding them on the basis of his calculations— so that many of the positions taken here under the name Einstein represent rather the effect he has on other physicists than his own specific views. In the quotation from his paper of 1916 given above where he speaks of Minkowski, note that it is only the "formal" equivalence of space-like and time-like coordinates which he adopts. In *Nature*, 1921, p. 783, Einstein says of time: "With respect to its rôle in the equations of physics, though not with regard to its physical significance, time is equivalent to the space coordinates (apart from the relations of reality)." In his essay of 1920 on "Aether und die Relativitäts-theorie," p. 15, he says: "Nach der allgemeinen Relativitäts-theorie ist der Raum mit physikalischen Qualitäten ausgestattet: es existiert also in diesem Sinne ein Aether. Gemäss der allgemeinen Relativitäts-theorie ist ein Raum ohne Aether undenkbar: denn in einem solchen gäbe es nicht nur keine Lichtfortpflanzung, sondern auch keine Existenzmöglichkeit von Massstäben und Uhren: also auch keine raümlich-zeitlichen Entfernungen im Sinne der Physik. Dieser Aether darf aber nicht mit der für ponderable Medien charakteristischen Eigenschaft ausgestattet gedacht werden, aus durch die Zeit verfolgbaren Teilen zu bestehen: der Bewegungsbegriff darf auf ihn nicht angewendet werden." Here he seems to return to the old need of a satisfying word, though denying to it all satisfying qualities.

On this phase compare Steinmetz' rejection of ether and his substitution of a field of force for it, defining such a field as "a condition of energy storage in space exerting a force on a body susceptible to this energy." *Four Lectures on Relativity and Space*, p. 18.

P. 22.   See Eddington, *Scientific Monthly*, January, 1923, p. 52 for the difference in the way in which Einstein's results affect old gravitation laws and old electro-magnetic laws.   Relativity, as it stands, does not affect number, action or entropy. Eddington, The *Mathematical Theory of Relativity*, p. 5.

P. 24.   Professor R. P. Baker of the University of Iowa suggests a situation under which exact agreement, as an ultimate aim, must be thrown out of consideration entirely.   I quote his interesting remarks:   "By writing $t = ict'$, the Lorentz transformation becomes a rotation in four dimensions. The special L transformations do *not* form a group.

"This means that if observers A, B, C, moving with relative velocities $(u_1v_1w_1)$ $(u_2v_2w_2)$ $(u_3v_3w_3)$ uniformly past one another did the Einstein light signalling act, and A reports that B's universe is transformed by L(AB), and B that A's is transformed by L(BA), these being inverse transformations, and we proceed to A's direct report on C, we find that this differs from the report that would be derived by compounding B's report on C with A's report on B; not an unusual affair in reports, but to my mind interesting to a sociologist, as suggesting the conceivability of universes in which agreement (exact) is impossible.   A similar thing occurs in music (equal tempered scale) due here to the false postulate $3^{12}=2^{19}$. The discrepancy above is reducible to a 'space rotation' of course very small for ordinary velocities and practically negligible. The only way to remove it completely is by using a group. The only one analytically available is the group keeping one set of generators of the absolute fixed. This is equivalent to compounding with the Lorentz transformation a complex transformation of space coordinates. Whether this is admissible or not depends on the possibility of a thoroughgoing complex physics. At present the price appears too high even for agreement."

### IV. Space

P. 26. See Chapter X for further discussion of language.

P. 32. Lewis, *Valence*, p. 163: "As far as we are aware the electrons cannot exist except in one of a series of levels; whether the idea of *motion* from one level to another has any meaning is somewhat doubtful. As far as we can see it disappears from one level and reappears at another."

### V. Time

P. 34. A hint at the time effect in our current picture of the world our language describes as real

can be secured at any moving picture show where
the pictures of some swift motion, as say that of a
galloping horse are slowed down, with the effect of
giving the animal a leisurely progress through the
air: or conversely where some slow motion is speeded
with likewise an effect of absurdity. Corresponding
hints of space effects can be secured from the commonly used illustration of the distortion of convex
and concave mirrors.

P. 35. On the rhythmic ta-ta of the brain-cells,
see Ehrenwald, *Archiv für die gesamte Psychologie*,
XLV, 144.

P. 36. The chess player illustration is used by
*Nordmann, Einstein and the Universe*, p. 75.

P. 37. For the space time of a dog, see A. Kap-
loun, *Journal de Psychologie*, 1923, p. 445, or Fries,
*The Monist*, 1921, p. 384.

P. 38. For the instantaneous, see Whitehead,
*Principles of Natural Knowledge*, p. 99, who says:
"There is no such thing as a molecule at an instant.
A molecule requires a minimum of duration in which
to display its character." The same author in his
work *The Principle of Relativity*, p. 7, says: "The
self-contradictory idea of an instantaneous event has
to be replaced by that of an instantaneous configuration of the universe. But what is directly observed
is an event. Thus a duration, which is a slab of

time with temporal thickness, is the final fact of observation. It is an essential assumption that a concrete fact of nature always includes temporal passage."

For simultaneity, see Birkhoff, "Origin, Nature and Influence of Relativity," *Scientific Monthly*, March 1924, who writes: "The one outstanding fact which must be granted before the new theory of relativity can be properly understood is that the notion of absolute simultaneity is not a self-evident truth, but implies a significant physical correlation of events."

P. 39. The physicist now calls the time as measured from any one point of reference, the proper time or the local time of that reference system. It is defined as the time of any one Galilean space for an observer in it. See Eddington, *Scientific Monthly*, Jan., 1923, p. 44. The relativity theory "in no wise tampers with the local instants which form the stream of our consciousness; it fully recognizes that the chain of events in such a time succession is a series of an entirely distinctive character from the succession of points along a line in space."

P. 39. Eddington, *Space, Time and Gravitation*, p. 52, plots the curves of the doubtful past and the doubtful future. See, also, Whitehead, *The Principle of Relativity*, p. 31.

P. 41. It is much easier to indicate the new reality of time than the old "reality" of common language. The view of the last few hundred years seems to have been that in time things have been "exactly so" in the past, but are not now: and will be "exactly so" in the future, but are not yet: with an infinite number of these "exactly so" stages both backwards and forwards—all as inspected, or at least capable of an "exactly so" inspection from the present. This seems to amount in substance to a very positive affirmation of the reality of certain parts of speech, the tense forms. The new view shifts the emphasis from the "exactly so" characterizations, because relativity finds no single pre-eminent point of view for determining them, but it gives much more body to durations as existing in temporal extension, and through the relativity of temporal locations and measurements, and the overlapping of durations, gives a body of reality to the full time progression. Compare *Revelations*, xiv, 13: "For their works follow with them."

P. 42. "Inside" the atom, the old time word, as well as the old space word meets its Waterloo.

## VI. Space-Time: Action

P. 44. Technically in his mathematics the physicist combines space and time by his assumption that one second equals 186,000 miles, the velocity of light in vacuum. The word "equals" has no ulterior meaning beyond indicating the fact that the two quantities, one of space and the other of time, work together in that way in space-time formulas. For the physicist this positing of one second equals 186,000 miles is the essential characteristic of the new relativity. For the non-physicist observer it is the essential characteristic of the new physics that is not "relative," joining in this aspect the other quanta mentioned in a later chapter.

Much interesting reading on the union of space and time will be found in Ouspensky, *Tertium Organum* and Korzybski, *The Manhood of Humanity.* Ouspensky puts his statement thus: A point moves in a direction not contained in it, that is, a line. A line moves in a direction not contained in it, that is, a surface. A surface moves in a direction not contained in it, that is, a solid. A solid moves in a direction not contained in it, that is, time, the fourth dimension. For his own purposes he goes on to say that time moves in a direction not contained in it, that is, eternity: but that extension is not within our province here. (See p. 35, *Tertium Organum.*) Korzybski describes man as the time-binding class of life, holding together past and future in one whole, as contrasted with plants which are chemistry-binding, and animals which are space-binding. His interests and purposes are likewise outside of our present province, but his discussion as well as Ouspensky's, may be mentioned to make concrete the new aspect of things to the reader. (*Manhood of Humanity*, p. 58.)

Add to these illustrations the following passage from H. G. Wells, *The Time Machine*: "Here is the portrait of a man at eight years old, another at fifteen, another at seventeen, another at twenty-three, and so on. All these are evidently sections, as it were, three-dimensional representations of his four-dimensional being, which is a fixed and unalterable thing." Quoted by Eddington, *Space, Time and Gravitation*, p. 45. And the following from Proust, *Du Côté de Chez Swann*, p. 60, 61: "Je m'avançais dans l'église, quand nous gagnions nos chaises, comme dans une vallée visitée des fées, où le paysan s'émerveille de voir dans un rocher, dans un arbre, dans une mare, la trace palpable de leur passage surnaturel, tout cela faisait d'elle pour moi quelque chose d'entièrement différent du reste de la ville: un édifice occupant, si l'on peut dire, un espace à quatre dimensions—la quatrième étant celle du Temps—déployant à travers les siècles son vaisseau qui, de travée en travée, de chapelle en chapelle, semblait vaincre et franchir non pas seule-

ment quelques mètres, mais des époques succes-
sives d'où il sortait victorieux."

For curious pre-Einstein speculations as to how
the world appearance would be changed for us with
slight alteration of single personal details, see Sir
William Crookes on the changes that would follow
in the appearance of all things from a simple change
in the height of the observer.  Also speculations of
William James, as to the effect if our lives were
short and swift or long and slow.  These and others
are described by G. Moch, *La relativité des phénomènes*, Chap. III.

P. 45.  Eddington says illustratively of the interval that "the time of which we are immediately
conscious is not in general physical time, but the
more fundamental quantity which we have called
the interval (confined, however, to time-like intervals)."  *The Mathematical Theory of Relativity*,
p. 23.

P. 46.  *Nordmann, Einstein and the Universe*, p.
78: "To be precise, the distance in time and the
distance in space between two contiguous events
are numerically to each other as the hypotenuse
and another side of a rectangular triangle are to
the third side which remains invariable."  This
fixed base of the triangle of which the other two
sides, the spatial distance and the chronological

distance, vary with the velocity of the observer, is invariant and is compared with the interval.

P. 47. Action. For discussion, see Eddington, *Space, Time and Gravitation*, p. 147. Russell, *The A. B. C. of Atoms*, p. 165, says: "Action turns out to be fundamental both in relativity theory and in the theory of quanta."

P. 47. Quanta. See Chapter VII following on Units and Limits.

P. 48. Events. See full discussion, by Whitehead, in his three books: *The Concept of Nature, The Principles of Natural Knowledge,* and *The Principle of Relativity.*

P. 48. The quotation from Minkowski is from his lecture on space and time, translated by Saha and Bose, *The Principle of Relativity*, p. 71.

Moritz Schlick, *Space and Time*, p. 66, writes: "Minkowski had enunciated his proposition in terse language that space and time in themselves are reduced to the status of mere shadows, and only an indissoluble synthesis of both has an independent existence. So on the basis of the general theory of relativity we may now say that this synthesis itself has become a mere shadow, an abstraction: and that only the oneness of space, time and things has an independent existence."

P. 48. Washington Monument. Whitehead uses

Cleopatra's Needle and Einstein uses Pottsdamer Platz for illustration.

## VII. Units and Limits

P. 51. For the new units of physics, see Russell, *The A. B. C. of Atoms*, Chap. XII.

P. 52. For the ratio of space curvature to the radius of the electron, see Eddington, *The Mathematical Theory of Relativity*, p. 154. For the large pure number constant, see same work, p. 167 (the ratio of the radius of an electron to its gravitational mass $= 3.10^{42}$).

P. 54. Planck. *A Survey of Physics*, p. 67, after showing the overthrow of the mechanical theories of nature, asks the question: "What is the real substance, what are the invariable elements, from which the whole universe is built up?": and proceeds to name in answer: "the so-called universal constants: chiefly the velocity of light in a vacuum, the electric charge and mass of an electron at rest, the 'elementary quantum of action' obtained from heat radiation and which probably plays a fundamental part in chemistry, the constant of gravitation, and many others."

## PART II

### The Position of Man

I wish to emphasize the statement that in the whole of Part II the discussion is solely critical. There is no effort to arrive at any statement of positive value, but only an effort to bring out clearly some of the worst difficulties with language which hamper all study of men in society. These obscurities, these crudely assumed realities behind the words, must be grappled with fundamentally by every student who wishes to make progress. To avoid the issue, to accept the words as they have arisen in current practical living, is to restrict the value of all the work that is done to the correctness of the assumption that these current practical words are adequate scientific descriptions and definitions.

### VIII.  Inside and Outside: Far and Near

P. 57.  The discussion of inside and outside, far and near, in the text will of course be inadequate and superficial to any mathematician or physicist who reads it. That is because the scientists have in so many ways undermined the common usages of these words, either leaving them with limited technical meanings or relegating them to the sphere of the wholly meaningless. My task is, however, as ever not to make a statement the physicist and the mathematician will like but to show the critical importance of their results when applied to the very crude obscurities still remaining in the terminologies about man and about society.

Upon the first use of a word like inside, the mathematician will point out to us that while in the older geometries a point P may be located inside a triangle, yet in the transformation of projective geometry there is no distinction of inside and outside in a plane. He will then proceed to show us a point A "inside" a Jordan curve (a closed curve, of which a circle is a type), which is inside the curve in the sense that no continuous path can connect the point A with a point B, "outside" the curve, without cutting the curve. And then he will add that the converse is *not* true: namely, that if A and B cannot be so joined it does not follow that a Jordan curve is the separator; the separating curve need not be closed, leaving us with the paradox to digest.

If we ask a physicist about a point "inside" an

atom, particularizing it as a point inside a sphere of which the center is somewhere in the proton and which includes all the valence electrons, he will proceed to define the electron in terms of its field which theoretically covers all space, and from that point of view leave us again without either inside or outside.

A simple illustration of the common confusion of inside and outside in ordinary space terms is seen in the relation of the sun to the earth's orbit. We say confidently enough that the sun is "inside" the orbit, at its center approximately—until we happen to remember the Ptolemaic system, which, considered as in a plane, puts the sun outside. The relative motions are the same in both cases. Dogmatically, common belief was Ptolemaic until the switch; and then with equal dogmatism common belief became Copernican. But in terms of relative motions before Copernicus and after, "inside" and "outside" are merely vague and valueless words.

P. 59. A most striking exhibit of what is happening to the inside and the outside, the far and the near, in the new physics is presented by Professor G. N. Lewis in his Silliman lectures at Yale University, December, 1925, of which brief abstracts are printed in *Science*, Dec. 18 and Dec. 25, 1925. Dr. Lewis advances a new theory of light, suggesting that atoms do not emit light promiscuously into space, but only to other atoms. It is not "emission but transmission, in which the emitting atom and the receiving atom play symmetrical and equally important parts." Or in other words "what we do now determines whether certain light particles shall have left a star a thousand years ago although in ordinary parlance the star may meanwhile have disappeared." And again it means that under relativity and using the space-time interval instead of space alone or time alone parts at least of every star, no matter how remote in Euclidean distance, are within every observer. Or in Dr. Lewis' own words: "My eye touches the star not in the same sense but in just as truly a physical sense as my finger touches the table." On the time side it means, if the theory holds good, that the course of past events can be altered. Dr. Lewis develops his theory in connection with the reversibility or irreversibility of physical process, a subject to which Max Planck, has given much attention (see his *Survey of Physics*). Relativity means, Dr. Lewis argues, that the universe is not running down mechanically, but that it also winds itself up, that the chances can be calculated, and the return to an original state of high potential energy must ultimately take place.

Psychology and philosophy have for generations

worried over the problem of what would happen to the observed without any observer. Physics now approaches an analogous problem, but in an atmosphere of work not of worry.

P. 59. For a discussion of some of the many attempts to handle Zeno's problems, see Cajori, "The Purpose of Zeno's Arguments on Motion," *Isis*, 1920, p. 7.

P. 61. Silberstein calculates the radius of the universe as larger than this, namely 114,000,000 light years, raising the figure of the comparison in the text to about $10^{26}$. Address, Toronto meeting 1924, British Association for the Advancement of Science.

P. 62. Such terms as before and after, part and whole, as used in the study of society are subject to similar criticism to that given the terms inside and outside and far and near. They have been produced in social development for practical purposes, and their practical value does not justify us in letting them dominate the study of the very process that produced them.

### IX.  The Words "Matter" and "Mind"

P. 63. Professor Woodbridge's article, "Mind Discerned," *Journal of Philosophy*, vol. 18, may be read with profit. After quoting Santayana's characterization of mind phenomena as all phenomena that cannot be put in our space-time complex, he suggests the phrase, universe of discourse, as a clearer and cleaner term than world of phenomena or sum total of experience. The universe of discourse is fundamentally characterized for him by contrast of subject matter and interpretation which is always recurring and cannot be broken down.

### X.   Language and Epistemology

P. 65.   Watson, *Psychology from the Standpoint of a Behaviorist*, p. 310: "Man is a social being and almost from birth language activity becomes part of his every adjustment."   Also p. 316: "Thought is the action of language mechanisms."   For a full discussion of the bodily integration of thought, see Chapter IX of Watson's work, passim.   This trend of attitude is, of course, not yet generally followed by psychologists.   From the second edition of Watson's work, pp. 345–6, I may quote:   "We would not abstract language, overt or implicit, or other implicit thought processes, from their general setting in bodily integration as a whole."   Thought "is a constituent part of every adjustment process." "The term thinking ought to be made to cover generally all implicit language activity and other activity substitutable for language activity."

The more recent works on language by specialists

in that field tend very strongly towards this general view. Take for example Edward Sapir (*Language*, 1921), whose remarks are all the more significant because psychologically he tends to regard thought under the older and narrower definition forms. "Thought," he writes, p. 14, "may be defined as the highest latent or potential content of speech, the content that is obtained by interpreting each of the elements in the flow of language as possessed of its very fullest conceptual value." But as he continues he says, p. 16, "It is easier to understand . . . that the most rarefied thought may be but the conscious counterpart of an unconscious linguistic symbolism." And p. 232, "Language and our thought grooves are inextricably interwoven, are, in a sense, one and the same": and again, p. 239: "For thought is nothing but language denuded of its outward garb." All this positive testimony despite the fact that for him such words as consciousness and mind still have positive independent values.

From the delightful works of Fritz Mauthner, all too rarely quoted, many strong statements might be taken. In *Zur Sprache und zur Psychologie*, 1906, p. 193, he writes: "Die Sprache unterscheidet sich vom Denken so wenig als das Tuch woraus der Rock gemacht ist, sich vom Rocke unterscheidet," and pages 625–6: "Gedächtniss, Bewusstsein, Sprache sind drei Synonyme": "Die Worte, Seele, Selbstbewusstsein, Bewusstsein sind überflüssig, sinnlos." In Die Sprache, p. 87, he says: "Die Sprache ist ja sozial. In der Sprache ist, wie ich (Kritik der Sprache I seite 24 ff.) gezeigt habe, die äusserste Utopie des Kommunismus Wirklichkeit geworden."

Ogden and Richards in *The Meaning of Meaning*, do not commit themselves as to the respective "meanings" of thought and language: they do not need to, they get a better audience without, and their whole book is indeed an argument against dogmatism about such terms; but in a footnote, p. 19, they write: "Whether symbols in some form or other are necessary to thought itself is a difficult problem, and may be postponed . . . Whether or not thought can proceed without symbolization it is certain that its recording and its communication (telepathy apart) require symbols . . . In the normal case the actual development of thought is very closely bound up with the symbolization which accompanies it." Not so much on the cautious phrasing of this quotation as on the whole tenor of their investigation I am inclined to think their actual working principle is about the same as that to be taken in this book. Whether a dogmatic statement by me would agree with one by them I do not know, for I have none to make: what theirs would be, if for any purpose they happened to want to make one, does not concern the question at issue.

P. 67. Mauthner Kritik der Sprache, 2d ed. I, pp. 11–12, discusses early ideas of the origin of language, whether handed down by a law-maker, or being a natural growth, these early ideas having usually no content or implication beyond a particular language. So far indeed from language being a subject for mythology, it is more accurate to define all mythologies as within language, forming a special interpretative system within it.

P. 70. The most valuable book in the field of language and epistemology is that of Charles K. Ogden and I. A. Richards, *The Meaning of Meaning*, 1923. I regret that I did not know of it in time to make use of it in the text.

P. 70. It may be remarked that it has long been common to refer to mathematics as the most perfect form of language. At the same time we are accustomed to think of the mastery and advance of mathematics as the most difficult accomplishment of thought. The running together of these two forms of remark is worthy of notice in this connection.

P. 71. For the consolation of any one not liking

the intimate union of thought, language, society and reality, I take pleasure in reprinting a few sections from the work of Mr. A. B. Johnson, *Harper and Brothers*, 1836, entitled "A Treatise on Language or the Relation which Words Bear to Things," Lecture 2.

"I cannot teach you," writes Mr. Johnson, "the relation that words bear to created existences, till you can contemplate the existences apart from words."

§ 1.  "Creation is boundless, whether we estimate its objects numerically, or its extent superficially. We cannot by penetrating the earth, discover a vacuity: we cannot exalt our vision beyond created objects: we cannot fathom the fullness of the ocean.

§ 2.  "To bring this immensity of existences within our definite comprehension naturalists divide the whole into a vegetable kingdom, a mineral kingdom and an animal kingdom: with various subdivisions of classes, orders, species, etc.

§ 3.  "Chymists subject creation to a still more concise classification. All objects are convertible, chymically, into about forty different substances: and chymists classify objects with reference to the subjects into which they are thus convertible: hence with chymists the universe is reduced into about forty different substances.

§ 4. "To understand the relation which words bear to created existences, we must contemplate creation apart from words. Creation is susceptible of a classification more definite, and even less multifarious than that of chymistry. This classification will constitute the present discourse.

§ 5. "The eternal universe may be divided into sights, sounds, tastes, feels and smells.

§ 11. "We must discriminate between the extent and variety of creation and the paucity of language.

§ 21. "Words are confounded with things."

## XI. Consciousness and Man

P. 73. How trial and error is a procedure prominent not only in evolution and in animal behavior, but through all human mental life including æsthetic and intellectual, is brought out at length by W. B. Pillsbury, *Revue Philosophique*, vol. 96, p. 202.

P. 73. Saunders, "Some Aspects of Modern Spectroscopy," *Science*, LIX, p. 50: "Certainly it seems painful to conceive, as C. G. Darwin puts it, of an electron with knowledge of the future, so that while leaping from one orbit to another it determines in advance the frequency with which it would be appropriate to radiate, taking into account its final destination." This article formed the address of the vice president of the physics section of the American Association for the Advancement of Science, at the 1923 meeting.

P. 75. Watson, *Psychology from the Standpoint of a Behaviorist*, preface, says of consciousness and the other terms mentioned: "I frankly do not know what they mean, nor do I believe that anyone else can use them consistently." Compare Pillsbury, *Philosophical Review*, vol. 26, p. 68, in his article on "New Developments in Psychology," for his discussion of the recent school of psychologists that wipes consciousness off the slate altogether.

In the second edition of his book (1924) Watson writes: (p. 3) "Consciousness with its structural units, the irreducible sensations (and their ghosts, the images) and their affective tones, and its processes, attention, perception, conception, is but an indefinable phrase. Also p. viii, "If behaviorism is ever to stand for anything it must make a clean break with the whole concept of consciousness." Fritz Mauthner contributes this, *Kritik der Sprache*, 2d ed., I, p. 650, "Der Begriff Selbstbewusstsein wird auch' von' unseren wissenschaftlicheren Psychologen geführt, so wie die Landapotheken Schlangenfett und dergleichen weiterführen. Weil die Bauern es verlangen."

P. 75. The definition quoted is from Sabin, "Giving Up the Ghosts," *Journal of Philosophy*, 17, p. 708.

# PART III

## Our Knowledge of Society

So far as extracts from current sociological writings are criticized herein, it is for illustrative purposes merely. The quotations may not always be fair to the wider attitude of the authors. Believing that all sociology is tending towards a unified coherent statement of social fact, it is my aim to get nearer to the point of view that is common to the most thorough investigations. The passages criticized are in general those that present conflicting aspects that seem to me hurtful and in need either of elimination or else of relinquishment while waiting fuller knowledge.

## XII. Man-Society

§ 1. The word society has no agreed meaning among sociologists. Each specifies it for some limited purpose of his own, while it remains at the same time for all a blanket term for a wide range of facts. Typical is the fact that in limited meanings there is no agreement as to what the earliest evolutionary phenomena are which may be called social. As against the varied sociological uses, it is interesting to note that behaviorist psychology inclines to let the social appear soon after behavior itself. The word is, of course, exact in its meaning in many special practical uses. It may have a legal definition for a particular form of organization. As organized pleasuring it may be so definite in some particular locality as to permit an exact count of heads. The reason such uses are definite is that each of them points to some particular group activity in the wider society. When we pass to the use of the term in contrast with such other terms as community, nation, state, group, institution, custom or culture, we have complete confusion, and apparently no prospect of agreement.

§ 5. An excellent illustration of the accurate use of the word group may be found in J. Vendryes, *Language*, pp. 240 ff. "Language" says Vendryes to start with, "is the strongest of bonds uniting a group." Here he thinks of the group very concretely as so many men in such a territory, but he quickly gets away from this. Victor Henry in his Antinomies Linquistiques, 1896, had been the first

to make it clear that language must be envisaged
generally as something that was substantially identical for all people at one end of the scale, and yet
different for every individual man at the other,
showing that if one took all the various peoples of
the world with all their languages, still they all had
one speech; while on the other hand if one took two
Parisians of the most exactly similar position, situation, training, experience, nevertheless the two had
different speeches; that while every individual had
a different language, yet there was in just as true
a sense one language for all men.  Appreciating
this, as do all students of language today, Vendryes
shows us first languages territorially spread, and
then languages occupationally spread.   From this he
passes to special languages, those employed by
groups of individuals placed in special circumstances,
as for instance law language, ecclesiastical, poetical,
the special Greek chorus language, scholar's Latin,
slangs, argots.   He discusses two brothers living together but practicing different trades, and the way
their language developments change as they move
out into their trade lives each day and move back
into common intercourse each night.   After having
placed language in the group, he says:  "But we
have yet to define the group.  In a word this will
be the object of the ensuing chapters."   And what

he comes to is that the language as specified at each stage and characterized or named at that stage, is the group as such-and-such activity so isolated for consideration and so specified. Consider these further statements of Vendryes in the same connection: "Language being a form of activity has a practical purpose, and we must study it in its relation to the whole of human activity—to life itself." And then: that this life is "the sum of those conditions in which humanity moves and has its being." (P. 234.)

### XIII.  The Social Fact

§ 6.  See sec. 68 concerning pedagogical tests in the organization of the material.

§ 13.  I have given no separate treatment to the social mind, nor to theories of social psychology, nor to any of the older super-individual structures. If it be true that we can analyze a law or a governmental process or an idea process in terms of activity in man-society, then all of these old structures fall away.  See comment to section 57, following.

By way of illustration take first the three senses for the term Social Mind which M. M. Davis finds in his "Psychological Interpretations of Society," *Columbia Studies in History Economics and Public Law*, vol. 33, No. 2, p. 49.  These are:

1.  The common mental possessions of a society.

2.  The common mental qualities of the individuals within a society.

3.  A certain sort of common consciousness to be called social consciousness which is an efficient dynamic agent in social action.

As to these we may only need to note the terms "common," "mental," "qualities," "individuals" and "consciousness" all of them undefined and very vague. Mr. Davis concludes (p. 73) that "the dynamic agent of the psycho-social unity is the social mind, a mass of common beliefs, sentiments and determinations possessed by the individuals of a group with the added consciousness that the other members simultaneously cherish them."

Very different in its results is the discussion given by R. B. Perry in his two articles, "Is there a Social Mind?" in the *American Journal of Sociology*, vol. 27, and in his article, "Is Society a Person?" *Journal of Philosophy*, February, 1924. After a careful analysis of such words as class, whole, individuality, system, compound and personality, Mr. Perry concludes that there is no social mind as a new being of higher order, and that society is not a person with the values of individual personality; and he does it in a way to destroy the evil influences on the society side of the opposition, and to undermine those on the individual side. His own interest, however, remains with individual personality and does not reach to the interpretation of the functioning process of society in which lies the interest of students.

On the basis of the old practical bifurcation of mind and matter a good common sense judgment is reached by W. F. Ogburn, "The Historical Method in the Analysis of Social Phenomena," *Publications of the American Sociological Society*, XVI, p. 74. "In segregating and measuring the two factors, the cultural and the psychological that are present in all social phenomena," he writes, "the first step is to determine the cultural factor, which is commonly done by the historical method. The psychological factor can only be seen clearly after the cultural factor is known and the historical setting is understood. If the attempt is made to determine the psychological factor before the cultural factor is known, the probability of error is generally so great as to make it untrustworthy."

The above conclusion he describes as a methodological rule of guidance which is of the utmost significance and the greatest vitality, and the principal idea of his paper. I am, of course, heartily in sympathy with his trend as an investigator, but I have not the slightest idea, and cannot get by the most careful reading of his paper, the slightest idea of what he means by the psychological factor, other than certain unanalyzed terms taken from psychological text books and every-day conversation. He himself says (p. 78) "Knowledge of the psychological factor depends upon a knowledge of psychology. For if we did not know psychology, we would not recognize the psychological factor when a historical analysis uncovered it." He seems to me merely to use psychological terms to satisfy his postulate that "there are two factors, the cultural and the psychological in all social phenomena, as illustrated by the relationship $x + y = z$" (p. 75).

I strongly recommend the study of such a paper as Mr. Ogburn's with these questions in mind: Is there anything described as psychological which is not just as susceptible of statement under the cultural descriptions as is anything described as cultural? Will not the term cultural fully cover all the phenomena brought into consideration?

One may note for incidental bearing that in the *Psychological Index* it has not been found practical to separate Race Psychology and Anthropology in the classifications. A discussion bearing upon this will be found in the *Journal of Philosophy*, "Psychology and Scientific Methods," vol. 17, pp. 345-9, by Madison Bentley, editor of the *Index*.

## XIV. Cross-Sectional Activity

§ 16. It is, of course, to be understood that I am not making any study of the Volstead law, and not seeking either any balanced statement of the facts or completeness of facts, much less making any judgment upon them. I am only pointing out some of the typical groupings to be found here, and doing it in rough terms of uncertain meaning, but the best available for the purpose. The use of such a term as "pleasure custom" does not connect for explanation purposes with pleasure as a matter of individual psychology, but is a social description.

§ 18. Compare Durkheim's early declaration that no social fact may be explained except in terms of other social facts. *Les Règles de la Méthode Sociologique*, p. 177: "Nous avons fait voir qu'un fait social ne peut être expliqué que par un autre fait social." See, also, Chapter XX of the present book.

§ 19. For the suggestion of many dimensions in mind, see Holt in *The New Realism*, p. 372.

In connection with this way of visioning society as groupal activities rather than as summary of individuals, one may recall the attitude commonly ascribed in sociological studies to the people of early times towards themselves and their society. One of the first things that struck investigators at

the beginning of the modern sociological development was the setness of early societies, the absorption of the individual in his community, the community tests and standards that appeared to be
dominant there as contrasted with the individual
tests and standards that seemed to be dominant in
our own times. Now without taking sides on this
question in terms of the comparative attitude of
individuals towards society then and now in a full
man-society statement, there is no question but
what the expression systems in the two periods are
in sharp contrast. In taking a cross-sectional view
of society we are therefore making an expression
having much in common with the immediate early
expression of man about his social life.

In considering the possibility and practicability
of this cross-sectional expression we must remember
that we today stand in a period of extreme highly
individualized expression. What we call "our"
western civilization is characterized by this great
emphasis on personality, in contrast not only to
early time but to other types of "civilizations" today. Now if we start forthwith by an assertion
that our western civilization is in this phase as in
all others at the very pinnacle of progress, and beyond
all question headed in the right direction, then the
cross-sectional statement will be rejected, of course,

as absurd. But if we remember (see section 105 following) that our own standpoint is not inevitably the best guide in valuing all standpoints in society, then we can begin to consider the practical value of cross-sectional expression fairly on its own merits.

Oriental nations have had much more feeling than we of the continuity of men, at least across the generations. Said Schamseddin at the gate of the tomb, lamenting his approaching death without posterity: "Tu t'eteintras, et il sera de toi comme si jamais tu n'avais été." "Les Mille Nuits et une Nuit: Grain-de-beauté." (Mardrus.)

## XV. Representative Activity: Governmental

§ 26. For interest groups, see sections 59 and 71 following. Also see Bentley, *The Process of Government*, 1908.

In connection with the variety of organization forms and procedures of representative nature in government, one may profitably examine the agricultural bloc in its various stages of development and subdivisions in Congress, 1920–1924. In current discussion we find the bloc attributed to demagoguery, and to arrant selfishness on the part of a class, we sometimes find it described as a germ of destruction for our representative government. The slightest analysis shows that a bloc on the floor of Congress differs only in technical details from similar groupal process in the cloak rooms or in lobbying organizations outside. It shows it in all important respects comparable to all the rest of present process of legislation, with development running back into the first years of the republic. Not on the lines of current criticisms, but in terms of publicity versus secrecy, in terms of party weakness versus party caucus power, and in terms of the particular sections of the population represented, will the true marks of differentiation in it be discovered. Also praise and criticism of it in every case will be reducible to cross-sectional activity represented; and the more blatant and violent the criticism or praise, the "rawer," so to speak, will be the character of that representation.

§ 27. Compare the articles by A. Gordon Dewey, "On Methods in the Study of Politics," *Political Science Quarterly*, Dec., 1923 and July, 1924. Also the article "The Behavior of Legislative Groups: a Method of Measurement" by Stuart A. Rice, *Political Science Quarterly*, March, 1925, pp. 60–72, in which the author, studying legislative votes, suggests two indexes, one of cohesion within groups, and one of likenesses between groups.

§ 29. Theories of sovereignty furnished the center

of the older political science, though quite properly they tended to describe themselves as political philosophy, rather than science. Their value was given them in this very description as dependent entirely on the value of the theory of the individual out of which and in opposition to which they reflected themselves. Sovereignty was supposed to exist somewhere, as such. It had its agents but it could not be defined in terms of their procedure, nor of the procedure of any other portion of society. It was a verbalism supposed to point very positively to some ultimate reality. It has proved by continuing study to be a verbal unreality. What the word was supposed to point at has been revealed in the very function of the activities of man-society as the study of them has continued. Laski in his voluminous writings is an easily available writer who makes some approximation to these positions, though with imperfect understanding. He is limited by the control of psychological terminologies exterior to his subject matter, by a continuing sense of need to orient himself with reference to standard theories of historical interest, but not fully functioned into our understanding of the life from which they arose, and above all by his dominating practical interests, which make his writings, like so many others, a hybrid between clear theory and clear practice.

## XVI.   Representative Activity: Opinionative

§ 30.   The following quotation from the preface to Professor Charles E. Merriam's *American Political Ideas* shows well the range of material that must be gone over in interpreting ideas:

"The purpose of the writer is to trace the broad currents of American political thought in their relation to the social, economic and political tendencies of the times.   Sometimes these ideas have best been expressed in political institutions: sometimes in laws, judicial decisions, administration or customs: again in the utterances of statesmen and publicists or leaders of various causes: sometimes by the formal statements of the political philosophers.   This study traces the main lines, the typical forms of political ideas in their relation to each other and to the conditions out of which they grew.   Some of these doctrines are thinly disguised pleas for group interests: others are parts of the great process by which the experience and counsel of the leaders, statesmen and sages are woven into the web of social and political control: others are relatively impartial and technical studies of social or political science.   All are individually parts of the progressive adaptation of democratic ideas to new economic and social conditions."

Professor Merriam's study is objective, his welcome to information from whatsoever source is catholic, he is fortunate in hampering himself with no set sociological scheme developed from individual psychology, and yet would he not benefit if his investigations could be made within a frame of definite functional meanings for such terms as he uses above, ideas, interests, groups, institutions, utterances, leaders, social control?

The entire purpose of the present essay may be said to be to participate in forming such a frame of meanings, drawn out of the material under examination, and lending itself within the range of that material to its better analysis.

§ 32. If we compare the treatment of public opinion and its relation to government as developed in the text, with such acute studies in the same field as for example those of Walter Lippmann, especially in his latest books, *Public Opinion* (1922), and *The Phantom Public* (1925), we see at once that it is not at all a question of one form of statement being wrong and the other right. We have statements in two frames of reference. Lippmann's form is valid enough for his purposes, his particular time, place, audience and range of problems. But generalizing the study it does not cut deep enough even on the comparatively superficial levels of psycho-analysis, much less on the deeper levels now becoming available to investigators. What is necessary is merely a transformation akin to the well-known transformations of the new physics, by which relations given in one form of reference can be restated in another of wider applicability.

§ 33. Suppose someone states the opposition of Catholicism and Protestantism as a matter of belief. It is at once apparent that that statement is only a tag or label for very many different things. The councils and creeds of the early church tell it. The History of the Reformation, which cannot be told except in terms of nationalities and politics and government and of the activities behind these, tells it. The various anti-Catholic movements in the United States tell it. The same thing is shown in the attitude of the present Russian government,—as it is variously misrepresented,—towards religion; and in the civil war splits among Protestant churches; and it is seen in germ in inchoate movements within the Protestant churches today.

This is not to deny that the specialized organization can be studied and analyzed for itself, not that the creeds and variations of creed can be so specialized and studied. But it is to say that even the baldest issue of Fundamentalist and Modernist within any Protestant church today gets its meaning, when we examine it right where it exists, in man-society, in a thousand other issues which must be taken into account, and some of which must be brought out into full prominence in connection with it, before we have it properly described.

§ 34. Fixed opinions and ideals may be said to be the correlates of metaphysical elements in the physical sciences, like the old space and time. Absolute space and time, from Newton on, and the ether, more recently, have been shown to have been merely words that satisfied the physicists' need of gumming together facts that did not need such gumming when better understood. So the fixed opinions and the ideals orient the puzzled man in his puzzling world without having other value than that. That that value is always transitory is now clear enough. The science of society, as opposed to metaphysical elements in its interpretation, will accept the ideals and opinions as first approximations to statements of facts and by interpreting them get at better statements of facts. Their values become functional throughout.

## XVII. Actor and Environment within the Social Fact

§ 35. The argument here is in no sense directed against the distinction of actor and environment as used by a psychologist for his purposes. Watson,

*Psychology from the Standpoint of a Behaviourist,*
p. 10, says: "The goal of psychological study is
the ascertaining of such data and laws that, given
the stimulus, psychology can predict what the response will be: or, on the other hand, given the response, it can specify the nature of the effective
stimulus." As postulates he takes: "Stimulus is
always given by the environment or body," "Responses always follow relatively immediately." His
postulates are entirely proper for his investigation.
But they do not control other investigations. The
substance of stimulus and response is social and
can be given coherent social statement.

Holt, The Freudian Wish, p. 167, defines behavior
as "any process of release which is a function of
factors external to the mechanism released." On
p. 202 he puts the query: "Why does a boy go
fishing?" Referring first to the old "bead" theory
of previous mental states determining the present
states, and next to the teleologic theory of ideas of
end in the mind determining action, he passes to
behaviorism, in terms of an integration of responses;
"The behavior of the growing organism," he says,
"is so far integrated as to respond specifically to such
an environmental object as fish in the pond." This
gives the approach of psychology.

For the approach of sociology we, however, face

directly a "groupal fishing activity participated in" to be accepted under the new durational and extension experience forms. Building up from the atom to the man was one thing, but building up from the electron—in its new aspects—to the man is very different. Building back and forth from the electron in its new aspects to the social facts directly envisaged is more in line. Which is to say that "groupal fishing activity participated in" is not merely direct primary observation, but is justified from the general methodological aspect of present science.

§ 39.  To illustrate the possibilities of cross-sectional as contrasted with psychological statement, the following report may be made on a series of conversations, half a dozen in number, primarily between two men whom we will call "A" and "B," but in the presence of small groups of participants varying in membership. The subject had to do with the selective factors in the establishment of friendships. "A" was a specialist in friendships and had his terminology on the lines of personal qualities and personality well in hand. "B" endeavored to cover "A's" views without his terminology, and he did not enter the first conversation until "A" had pretty fully worked out his personal position in interchange with the other persons present. When "B" started he said that he would attempt to restate the position "A" took without psychological phrasings. "A" did not catch that remark, and when "B" stopped, broke out at once: "But that is just what I have been saying." Such acceptance was all well enough for casual conversational purposes, but the matter was not quite so simple. The subject kept recurring, and after a week or two, when interest was exhausted, "B" drew up the following memorandum with which "A" was, in general, in accord:

1. We can approach this problem solely in terms of verbal "frames of reference"; i.e., specially organized sub-languages, designed for efficient description for specifically defined purposes and comparable therefore to the languages of mathematics, chemistry, theology, etc. The slightest attempt to assert any rightness in the reference the words have to a further reality, destroys the problem itself.

2. The problem then becomes whether friendship and friend-selection can most adequately be described in a closely purified language of individual psychology, or in a closely purified language of social experiencings.

3. Neither disputant thus far shows complete success in restricting his vocabulary to his announced scheme.

4. The particular problem, however, would seem

to be one of the easiest for the psychological vocabulary, and one of the hardest for the cross-sectional.

5. With increased care, either system of language may be expected to handle the complete situation.

6. Where the interest is in understanding the given friendships or antipathies in their full social setting, the cross-sectional statement will be most efficient.

7. Where the desire is every-day interchange of views, the psychological statement will be simpler, quicker, and brighter, and rank as the best shorthand of communication.

8. Each system of expression will improve in efficiency, the more fully it defines itself with reference to the other.

9. Any description which uses terms of wavering character, is unclear as to the two types, or supplements one by the other would appear to be confused and full of troublesome problems.

§ 41. In illustration of the absurdities that arise in lifting certain forms of psycho-analytical theory concretely for use as interpreters of society, one may examine Kolnai, Psycho-Analysis and Sociology. Typical passages are: "Anarchism is the faithful social projection of the uterus with repudiation of the manifest uterus-wish" (p. 116). "Bomb-throwing is an entirely mystical individual, unsophisticated

copy of parricide" (p. 122).  And more generally:
"Psycho-analysis testifies to the effect that the man-
ifestation of this universal wish (i.e. the uterus-
wish) of the struggle that is carried on against it,
and of the resultant compromises, constitutes the
most widely diffused content of collective ideas, and
is at the same time the chief sustainer of homogene-
ity."  One cannot help remarking on the fact that
such a book is deemed worthy of translation and re-
publication in English.  For similar vagaries, though
more respectable, see Otto Rank, *The Myth of the
Birth of a Hero*, and compare Otto Rank and
Hanns Sachs, *The Significance of Psycho-Analysis
for the Mental Sciences*.  An attempt to apply
psycho-analysis to the full groupal process of society
is made by T. D. Eliot, *The American Journal
of Sociology*, 26, p. 332, in his article "A Psycho-
analytic Interpretation of Group Formation and Behavior."  The study of such an article is profitable
to bring out clearly just what type of technical satisfactions it provides the investigator.  See, also, Park
and Burgess, *Sociology*, pp. 478–90.

§ 42.  "We can say almost with certainty, that
a given picture must have been painted at Siena,
such another at Florence or Venice or Perugia, and
when the reasons for these distributions are given,
it is quite evident that the several pictures came from

these and could not have been painted in any other localities. But in the craft of writing our literary senses have not been so minutely trained in critical examination. Locality does not only influence one's accent: it subtly shades all our perspectives and preoccupations: it should be found in every book, so that, after a few lines of any author, one should exclaim,—a Dublin book, a Connemara book, as one says at a taste or a smell—a Cheshire cheese, a Limerick ham, a Dublin Bay herring." James Stephens, *The Dial*, April, 1924. Compare what Jane Harrison read out of a fragment of a hymn of the Kouretes, as she developed it in her book "Themis," interpreting through it the social life of a long gone age. The influence of Durkheim upon her interpretation is specifically recognized by her.

To say that I have envisaged social facts in the manner of the text for twenty-five years is no more significant than perhaps to say I had seen a ghost that long ago and still believed in it. To say that I have developed it in fifteen years of the superficial contacts with society given by newspaper work has not much greater importance, for it is entirely too easy for an attitude towards fact to clot or crystallize and turn everything perforce into its own terms. But in my volume, *The Process*

*of Government,*[1] will be found, I believe, certain
fruits of this attitude on such topics as sovereignty,
the classification of government, the powers of government, political parties and public opinion, that
are not at all out of line with the recent trend of
political science.   For a discussion of recent theory
of this nature, see Barnes, *Sociology and Political
Theory*, 1923.   The earlier publication to which I
am referring, was not, however, primarily an effort
to come to clear vision on the problems above mentioned, the emphasis of the study being on the
"process," not on government directly, except as
material in that field was most easily available to me.
Similar studies in economic fields are more difficult
because of the clouding of all facts by the elaborate
technical theories and terminologies, which are all
governed, however obscurely, from practical groupal
points of view, without sufficient struggle to break
down fully the underlying terms and assumptions.
See the remark in Section 72 on the representative
value of such economic terms as rent, interest, etc.

[1] The University of Chicago Press, 1908.   An earlier effort in this
direction had been made in my article "The Units of Investigation
in the Social Sciences, Annals of the American Academy of Political
and Social Science, 1895, pp. 915–941.   Society was there conceived as a "nexus of actions" (p. 917), but the opposition to environment was still maintained, and the analysis wandered away
under the bonds of the common psychological terms in use at that
date.

There is in Germany at the present time a strong movement to give sociological interpretation to economic terminologies, that is, to review all economic theory in the light of the broader investigations called sociological. See especially the works of Gottl-Ottlilienfeld and their discussion by Hero Moeller in *Schmoller's Jahrbuch*, 47, pp. 273–82.

The very location of the present effort at social interpretation, it may be remarked, can be stated only in terms of man-society activities, in which it holds its representative position, however poorly or however well. The statement, I judge, would run something like this. Our groupal activities are under rapid change, and in a state of sharp conflict. They are throwing up their governmental and opinionative representative activities violently, and throwing them up into a field which possesses much new technical capacity to handle them. This process is bringing the opinionative activities, where they do not clot too crudely, to seek their respective valuations in terms of others. And there we are. They find their own relativity, their functional value, all the way along the line. Their representative activity heightens, let us hope, instead of lowers.

Is it not self-evident that such a statement, bare as it is, is vastly truer and richer than any set of remarks in questionable terms of doubtful meaning as to the mysterious processes taking place within the space limits of a particular suit of clothes in a certain month in such and such a township, county and state?

§ 43.  Compare Georgina Stickland Gates, *The Effect of an Audience Upon Performance. Journal of Abnormal and Social Psychology*, 18, 334.

### XVIII.  Human Nature as Environment

§ 44.  To any reader who does not like statements of the type of that in the first paragraph of this section and says he cannot understand them, I wish to say that he will not be any the worse off if he does not understand them.  I do not like them myself, but they answer to certain conventions in the discussion of such material, and if carefully made, have a value within their range.   I am very strongly of the opinion that there is no contribution of any science which is hard for any normal healthy person to grasp.  There are often enormous difficulties in the process of getting to it, and of following these processes as the scientist reports them to us.   But the difficulties both for the scientist and for his followers lie in breaking down old crystallized ways of interpreting, and more, of course, when we do not ourselves appreciate our subjection to them, than after we do appreciate it.   Einstein's way of looking at the universe is much simpler and more satisfactory than the old way. It is in that very simplicity that lies its value, and this is not simplicity for the mathematician and physicist alone: it is simplicity for everybody. That does not mean that I or you can get that simplicity in a moment, today or to-morrow. Our set forms must break down, of course, and sometimes it is hard. It is a case of the leopard and his spots. We know now that the leopard does change his spots, not any particular leopard at any moment, or even in his life span; but the family group leopard, the leopard in evolution. Our old space form, with its absolute measurement spots, its infinite spots, its boundary spots, is changeable; and changeable by a process vastly more flexible and speedy than the process of the leopard with his spots.

§ 48. The whole subject of instincts in relation to society is being very actively discussed at the present time, and the reader is referred to this readily available material.

William McDougall has perhaps staked the most in unhesitating submission to instincts as controlling factors. And there is no better test of the value of theoretical reliance on such factors than in the progressive deterioration of McDougall's output since his *Social Psychology*, through his Group Mind to his lecture series "Is America Safe for Democracy?" His system in *Social Psychology* consists of seven most important instincts, with reproductive, gregarious, acquisitive and constructive instincts appended for social uses, but with imitative, sympathetic and play instincts rejected. In two recent articles, one on "The Use and Abuse of Instinct," in the *Journal of Abnormal Psychology and Social Psychology*, Dec., 1921, and one entitled "Can Sociology and Social Psychology Dispense with Instincts?" in the *American Journal of Sociology*, May, 1924, he defends his position and in the latter article directs attacks on Professor Dewey's book *Human Nature and Conduct* and upon *Professor Knight Dunlap*. For criticism of the McDougall point of view, see the articles by Faris, "Are Instincts Data or Hypotheses?" *American Journal of Sociology*, 27, p. 184, and "Ethnological Light on Psychological Problems." *Publications of the American Sociological Society*, XVI, p. 113. See also Kantor, "The Institutional Foundation of a Scientific Social Psychology," *American Journal of Sociology*, May, 1924, and the discussions following this article and the McDougall article in the same number.

The volume on the *Original Nature of Man* by Edward L. Thorndike in his *Educational Psychology* should be examined and a book like Irwin Edman's *Human Traits and Their Social Signifi-*

*cance.* Mr. Edman assures us in his introduction that "We are almost unanimously assured by modern science" that "the native biological equipment of man, commonly known as human nature," has "remained substantially the same from the dawn of history to the present." His book is devoted to showing the various forms this native human nature is given by society, but it continuously assumes that this statement of "human nature" is the direct statement of the essential fact, and that, therefore, the real explanation of society is in terms of the human nature which society produces.

An interesting illustration may be found in Pierre Bovet's *The Fighting Instinct*, when the author studies the alleged instinct so described with a view to social control. What he wants to control is, of course, social fighting. The instinct, which is a descriptive term for the going activity is dragged in as a point of attack. He does not want to eliminate all the aggressiveness of going life, but the wars. In short he specifies what he wants to attack as an individual quality, and makes it his target. He has his values in his book, but they do not need that structure.

Of an older "human nature" breed is an advertisement in the *International Journal of Ethics*, Oct., 1918, by the president of the National Institution for Moral Advancement, asking for help in tabulating and analyzing "motives which impel human beings" in their conduct.

§ 50.   Studies into the social life of animals from the point of view of the activity of the animals themselves, have hardly begun except in such cases as those of ants and bees.   A suggestive article under the title "Have Sub-Human Animals Culture?" by Hornell Hart and Adele Pantzer appears in the *American Journal of Sociology*, 30, p. 703, in which modifications of the behavior of the higher mammals under domestication; and tradition and education in the song of birds, are considered.

§ 52.   For the use of human nature as a standard of values, see Thorndike's volume on the *Original Nature of Man* in his *Educational Psychology* under the heading, p. 310, "Original Nature the Ultimate Source of All Values."   Here this nature appears as the test of all progress.   Instincts, he tells us, "may be trusted to form desirable habits only under a strong social pressure whereby the wants of one are accommodated to the wants of all, but the most elaborate and artificial moral training which a social group prescribes is still ultimately an expression of man's nature."

It will be understood that the criticism in the text does not run to Thorndike's pedagogical or educational presentation, but to a strict cold question of technical explanation. Just as the physicist is free to use any one of the many frames of reference, according to his needs in his particular problem, so the worker in a special field of sociology, theoretical or applied, is free to choose his frame of reference which accords with the interpretational frames of his audience. The question here concerns entirely the relativity of that frame among the many frames.

Any one who cares to pursue the question further with a view to discovering what amount of accuracy can be secured in the use of terms like human nature and instinct, may compare Thorndike's positions with those of Bovet's book on *The Fighting Instinct*, mentioned above. Another profitable line of consideration will be found in the difficult problem of the origin of custom and law of incest. Take a series of writers on this subject; observe how far each of them goes until he introduces instinct; try to determine from his work just why he introduces instinct at the point he does; and then compare with them all Simmel's interpretation in terms of conditions of social living, *Soziologie*, pp. 660–665.

## XIX. Differences between Men: Birth and Death

§ 53. Osborn, Address at Columbia University, April, 1924, on "Cro-Magnon Culture. Watson,

*Psychology from the Standpoint of a Behaviorist,*
p. 12. "It lies well within the bounds of probability that if we were able to obtain a new born
baby belonging to the dynasty of the Pharaohs and
were to bring him up along with other lads of
Boston, he would develop into the same kind of
college youth that we find among Harvard students.
His chances for success in life would probably not
be at all different from his classmates."

What often happens in this field is readily illustrated from the Nordic literature. Nordic sym-
phonies are played on an instrument which has race
worshipper strings at one end and cranial study
strings at the other, with a full range between. At
one end the social meaning of value, the representative quality, can be very definitely traced down to
the groupal bearers. At the other end a set of very
definite and reliable observations in Euclidean space
and naïve time are spun out through positive psychologies and antiquated causations to presumable
conclusions. My assertions with reference to such
work become:

1. Not a bit of the writing but has social meaning and value.

2. Not a bit of the causation structure has any
value in the modern space-time background.

3. The would-be sociologist is not justified in

accepting this naïve material in its own system under the influence of its own naïveté.

4. The requirement for the sociologist is to float the whole of the naïve material in its social space-time setting and appraise it there.

5. And as to the Nordic in particular, he is as fictitious as a pagan god, a social whole or soul, or a technically personified individual man.

§ 54. The individual is sometimes described as the point of origin of innovation. But we must remember that "point of origin" is a phrase that has no meaning except as positing some originator outside the facts, and that not only innovation but every other social fact and aspect of fact is found only in the individual, down even to the deadest of what we call dead institutions. It is of no avail to appeal to inventions that do not get invented over again, for it cannot be assumed straightway that the explanation of this failure to reappear lies somewhere else than in any interpretation of man-society activity. This does not prove individual origination, any more than a showing of the much more striking assemblage of instances of multiple invention proves the contrary. Had Einstein died with his work unfinished, we cannot say whether it would or would not have been long before substantially the same work would have been accomplished. But whether

it would or would not have been long, has no bearing on the problem of whether our interpretation
is through a posited individual man or through the
intersectional statement of groupal activities.  For
a sociological criticism of the ordinary writings on
eugenics, see Warren S. Thompson, *Eugenics as
Viewed by a Sociologist, Publications of the American
Sociological Society*, 1923, pp. 60–72.

§ 56.  An interesting side-light on intelligence
tests is thrown by the case of a young man I know,
a college student.   Scarlet fever in his boyhood left
its mark in a slowing down of all procedure, so that
only with most dogged labor could he advance.   By
long determination he gained enough speed in one
sport, basket-ball, to become a good player, almost,
though never quite, up to the team requirements.
Always working, though always apparently lagging
in his work, he nevertheless held what he acquired.
By dint of various intelligence tests he got the hang
of them thoroughly.   Thus entering his second year
of college work he took his tests so well that he was
put in the first section of his class, and consequently
expected to do the heaviest work.   Very quickly he
fell behind his section and was unsatisfactory to
his instructors.   These latter, having positive and
convincing knowledge of his "intelligence" gained
from his high rank in intelligence tests, could admit

nothing but laziness or some other moral defect in him, and so made life a burden to him.  The point where intelligence tests fail is, of course, in a crude and unintelligent understanding of them by the test-givers who rely upon them.

§ 57.  The fact that I nowhere attack directly the individual man in the usual way, and discuss him systematically in relation to society, is of course due to my inability to hold the facts within the old terminologies and to my belief that they cannot be so held.  It may appear as a careless or conscious avoidance of an issue, that ought to be met squarely to start with; and this despite my frequent assertion that this is the very kind of an issue that must be postponed to the end; and not merely to the end of any man's work today, but to the end of much co-operative investigation, possibly across generations.

The general status of the present position may perhaps be sketched somewhat as follows.  Instead of starting with definite positions about individual and society, and with a mass of implicit or explicit positions on the bifurcations and loci examined in the test, we have a house-cleaning of these, and start directly with the complex of human society happenings.  We attempt our analysis in terms of analyzed portions of the observation, and not with previously postulated factors.  This does *not* put us

in the position of denying anything to the individual
as a phenomenon. It simply puts us in the position
of postponing determination about him.

Our observational report on the individual is then
something like this. Our early, socially speaking
eye-ear-touch-sense report on what is going on
around us gives us ourselves and other men separately. We do observe in generation and in re-
production phenomena in which these separate individuals are not separate, but the occasions are
transitory and we do not emphasize them. Later
our embryologists report facts of germ development
which also are outside of the common language
separateness, but for their purposes they do not
need to inquire into the meaning of this phase of
their observations. More recently still our psychologists and sociologists, though starting with individuals in environments have continously been
driven to ever wider social statement of the individual phenomena they are studying.

In this situation we therefore try systematically
what can be accomplished by a procedure that omits
entirely the social and individual categories as applied in a preliminary way to the sorting of our
materials, and that seeks to develop categories out
of the material itself, these of course being taken as
tentative, as what other sciences call first approxi-

mations, for use merely to see what value they may have to our study.

In this procedure we cannot be charged with ejecting the individual either phenomenally or ultimately from our field. We retain every bit of individual life, to use that form of description. We have the full material before us that the most extreme hero-worshipper has. We believe we have much more before us, but we certainly lose none of his.

We merely leave it for future study to show what the best description of these individual values as individual may prove to be. As for any further statement of these values in terms of personality, of soul, any one interested is as free to proceed on the basis of facts accumulated and stated under the present method, as he has been on the basis of facts accumulated and stated under the older method of every-day language, grammatical subject, predicate and object.

An interesting comparison of the contrasted statements, on one side that of current individualistic phrasings, on the other that of social activity, may be made by any reader at any time, out of the copious material furnished him by the newspapers on any event which is the leading sensation of the day. As this manuscript is being revised perhaps ninety per cent of the people of the United States and all of its newspapers, except perhaps one, are having an orgy over Chicago crime—if the courts indeed ultimately declare it a crime—in which two Chicago boys are reported as confessing in great detail to the kidnapping and murdering of a third. Let us assume the facts to be as the newspapers with surprising agreement as to detail, are reporting them.

Of journalistic importance are such aspects as the great wealth of the three families involved (placed combined, by common consent at $15,000,000), the business prominence of all three families, the fact that all three are of one religious-racial group, the educational precocity of the boys, the fullness of detail which was secured as to the long and careful planning of the crime, the unconcerned deliberateness with which killing was sought rather than avoided, the easy-going indifference with which the boys detached themselves from the crime before it was attached to them, and the equally easy-going indifference with which they furnished full details of it after it was attached to them, the distinguished conduct of the state's attorney, as in spending $102 for a single meal for the boys and for a party of investigators while preparing the case, and other aspects of that nature.

If one is making an investigation of idle hour entertainment in the present United States, all of this is very well. But if one weighs it for its importance in society, it will not stand very high, or if it has meaning of importance, that can only be found by carefully attaching it to other activities in society, and taking it in its expressive value with reference to them.

The crimes described, kidnapping to secure money, and murder are not uncommon. I am not sufficiently versed in the technique of such crimes to point out the more unusual details, but possibly the fact that the killing occurred by previous decision at the beginning of the crime, and the scheme to have the reward thrown out of the window of a fast train, might be selected. These are not great innovations, but merely variant details of such crime. The influence of Pietro Aretino, though worth many newspaper columns, can hardly compare with that of Nick Carter upon the youth of our land. The careful planning long in advance is common to many of our efficient professional criminals, and the present instance would not rank specially high in their annals. It would not rank at all high in connection with many other equally ruthless designs against the cash, happiness and lives of other people, found in other classes of operations not having this particular criminal label. The nonchalance of the murderers is not at all unusual, and gains its prominence only by contrast with what readers seem to expect from them at their age. So the criminal activity, like the journalistic activity, shrivels to small proportions when spread out and examined.

But now the crime has given occasion to a great number of expressions and discussions from teachers, preachers, psychologists and psychiatrists. Consider some of them. A teacher tells us that this is what higher education without a firm religious foundation brings to us. Another, joining with the many who stress egomania, points out that one university among all the universities of the land, is prominent for the egomania of everybody connected with it.

A preacher tells us that the weakening of the particular religious-racial home ties throws young men on uncharted seas and comes to this. A professor of philosophy points to the prevailing antinomianism in the land, which this illustrates. The head of a psychological laboratory combines prevailing egomania with a comparison with the ruthlessness of ordinary business life, in his comments.

A sociologist brings in the alien invasion and the resulting decline of national stamina, regardless of the fact that the young men, though foreign of surname, are of families of a stable type nationalized by seventy-five years of successful Americanism. A popular lecturer discusses flappers, short skirts and bobbed hair as symptomatic of conditions of which the crime is an outgrowth. The experts in insanity have much wisdom to reveal upon paranoia and other mental irregularities, though with great caution as to the case in hand. A psychiatrist at a convention of his fellows pleads for serious national consideration of the mental status of the population, and points with fear and trembling to a future in which "through ill-regulated immigration on the one hand and through the relatively insufficient fertility of the mentally superior stocks on the other, the general level of intelligence and character in the United States is bound to fall unless we take the necessary steps to prevent it."

In all these and in a thousand other variant comments we may separate three types of elements.

The interpretations in terms of antinomianism, egomania, and precocity are too thin for serious attention. They are merely ways of turning a bit of behavior into a psychological term which is supposed to explain them.

The interpretations in terms of physical and racial fitness are subject to very, very many assumptions as to the meanings of partially investigated facts. They also take social conditions as we find them and assume an adequacy of certain alleged physical differences among men to explain them, although these physical differences are known in the main only by inference from the social facts they are to explain. If the Cro-Magnon can be assumed to have had as much or even more intellectual capacity than we have today, we must certainly be cautious as to classifying our fellow men of today, and we may well remember "There goes John Wesley" when we interpret them under any particular conditions in which we find them.

The third type of element has to do with consideration in connection with other activities in man-society, stated with that particular value. A comparison with business methods and ideals under the tags of ruthlessness, and of "justification of means by ends" might be in order. An examination of the break-up of racial cohesion itself in terms of other activities might be in order. Even one with the conditions giving bobbed hair an ideal prominence as a form of behavior, or one examining journalistic stimulation.

And the value of such investigations is that when we have a preliminary statement we do not have a stopping point to our explanation that pretends to satisfy us, as we think we have when we have labelled a psychic quality; but instead we have a startini point for wider and wider interpretation in terms of the full net-work of activities. We have life, not death, in our interpretation, and we must and can proceed to get all the values and meanings related.

There is no difference in materials to start with. The dead boy and the live boys are before us, and all their acts. But also all the network of society that acts in them. The kidnapping in Euclidean space is so much matter-motion, perhaps, but in man-society which itself furnishes that Euclidean statement, it is just a specification of a kidnapping activity, traceable in its appearances and suppressions, through all the psychic technique and language technique it involves in terms of many other activities. We lose our cocksureness, but we gain— knowledge.

## XX.  Simmel: Durkheim: Ratzenhofer

§ 58.  If this chapter had to do with the creators of the science of sociology, perhaps the name of Karl Marx should be put at the head of the list. To my regret I am not sufficiently well acquainted with his work to untangle his theoretical from his practical achievement, and gain an opinion. Moreover I am not concerned with any estimate of permanent importance or place in history, a form of judgment for which I have no aptitude. It is here merely a question of getting the men who in the last generation have sought and built a theoretical unity of scientific social study. The name of Wundt is definitely excluded, for while Durkheim set up a social mind, comparable to Wundt's type of folk-soul, with Durkheim it was mainly a question of positing this social mind, much as Newton felt compelled for technical personal satisfaction to posit absolute space and absolute time, without actually using them in his system. Wundt's position is indicated by F. Mauthner, *Die Sprache*, p. 12. Comparing Wundt and Steinthal, he says the latter used the term Volksgeist, instead of Volksseele because he could not see a substance in it, whereas Wundt used the term Volksseele, because he felt in it a similar reality to the individual soul. "A similar unreality," Mauthner says, should have been the cue; and he adds that possibly that was what Wundt might really have meant after all.

The quotation from Simmel is from *Soziologie*, p. 17. "Es ist ja in geistigen Dingen nichts ganz Seltenes—ja auf den allgemeinsten und tiefsten Problemgebieten etwas Durchgehendes—dass dasjenige was wir mit einem unvermeidlichen Gleichniss das Fundament nennen müssen, nicht so fest steht, wie der derauf errichtete Oberbau."

§ 59.  Gustav Ratzenhofer, 1842–1904, an Austrian field marshal and administrator, with a hard positive personal acquaintance with the operating facts of the society around him, and a great freedom from the common sentimentalities of theory.

Wesen und Zweck der Politik, 3 volumes 1893
Die sociologische Erkenntniss              1898
Der positive Monismus                      1899
Positive Ethik                             1901
Die Kritik des Intelleks                   1902
Soziologie                                 1907
The Problem of Sociology, St. Louis Congress Arts and Letters, Vol. V.          1904

For discussion of his work, see Small, *General Sociology*, Chapters XII to XXVII.  What is practically an abstract of his entire system may be found in Gumplowicz, *Geschichte der Staats-Theorien*, pp. 446–491.

Ratzenhofer builds up in nature a physical-physiological-psychological series of the well-known type, and identifies different forms of interests along the line.  He knits these together as in the series from the sex interest through family, race, and wider social interests to what he characterizes as transcendental and religious interests.  (*Soziologie*, p. 17, pp. 78–9, p. 121.)  He speaks of inborn characteristics of races (Anlagen), but they are to him results of evolutionary experience of handling the environment in accordance with interests (*Soziologie,* p. 34). These Anlagen, like his Interessen, are therefore descriptive not interpretative. Consciousness and the intellect adapt themselves to the inherent interests, and the whole development of the creatures takes place in the sense of this subjective handling of experience. (*Die Kritik des Intellekts,* p. 24.)

He sums up his system in a passage in *Die Kritik des Intellekts,* p. 158, as follows:

"Nachdem wir den monistischen Positvismus als die philosophische Grundlage

die Verwertung des Interessengesetzes als die Methode der Soziologie

die Entwicklung als das Grundgesetz des Seins

die Anpassung des inhärenten Interesses als das Grundgesetz des menschlichen Wechselbeziehungen

das Socialgebilde als deren Einheit

den Daseinskampf auf Grund der Individualinteressen als die Form des socialen Verkehrs

die Auswahl unter den Geschlechtern auf Grund des Gattungsinteresses als das Element der Interessenübereinstimmung

und den absoluten und relativen
Zusammenhang aller Gesetzlich-
keit
erkannt haben, ist das sociologische
Problem nach jeder Richtung
gelöst."

The Social-gebilde, or institutions, which in the above passage are described as the unity of human interactions, are pictured in Part IV of the *Soziologie* and consist first of associations of blood, such as family, race and nobility: next institutions of power, then those of ideas, and finally those of civilization. The following passage (*Soziologie*, p. 143) may be quoted: "Die verschiedenartigsten Ideen können Sozialgebilde hervorbringen: die meisten derselben beruhen auf Sozialinteressen, wonach sich Menschen mit gleichen Bedürfnissen um das gemeinsame Ziel, die einigende Idee, auf Grund der Interessensolidarität zusammenschliessen. Doch kann sich ein solcher Zusammenschluss auch auf dem Boden des Individual- und Transzendental-interesses ergeben, indem gleiche Ziele die Menschen einen, auch wenn sie für jeden nur Sonderziele sind. Die Gesamtheit jener, die für die leitenden Ideen tätig sind, bildet einen 'Gesellschaftsverband.' Ausserdem aber gibt es Ideen, welche gewissen Personenkreisen eine bestimmte Stellung anweisen. Hier macht

nicht die eigene Idee ihre Träger zu einem Social-
gebilde: dasselbe lebt vielmehr von der wirklichen
oder vermuteten Bedeutung, die es für seine soziale
Umgebung besitzt. Hierbei ist stets vor Augen
zu halten, dass die niedern Interessen in letzter
Linie der Grund auch der höchsten, diese gewisser-
massen das Mittel zum Zweck sind: und dass Ideen
die scheinbar von höchsten Interessenformen ent-
springen, auch von den Massen durch instinktives
Erfassen des Zusammenhangs mit ihren niedern
Interessen geteilt werden können."

§ 60. Emile Durkheim, 1858–1917, professor at
the Sorbonne, editor of *L'Année Sociologique,* and
leader of the most important school of investigators yet gathered together in sociology.

| | |
|---|---|
| De la Division du Travail social | 1893 |
| Les règles de la méthode sociologique | 1895 |
| Le suicide | 1897 |
| Représentations individuelles et repré-<br>sentations collectives (Revue de Méta-<br>physique et de Morale) | 1898 |
| The Elementary Forms of Religious Life | 1912 |

Two discussions of his work in English will be
found in the *Philosophical Review,* Vol. 29, one by
Laguna on "The Sociological Method of Durkheim," the other by Schaub on "A Sociological
Theory of Knowledge." An extended treatment is

that of Gehlke, "Emile Durkheim's Contributions to Sociological Theory," 1915. Goldenweiser criticizes the book *Religion* at length in the *Journal of Philosophy*, 1917. Probably the best statement of Durkheim's position is, however, that of his associate, Halbwachs, *Revue Philosophique*, May, 1918. Halbwachs sums up Durkheim's work as follows (p. 410): "The great initial discovery of Durkheim was that social facts were specific and *sui generis*. In the field of investigations bearing on man, which appeared entirely occupied by the various social sciences, he succeeded in opening up a new region which he made the domain of a science."

Durkheim's definition of the social fact (*Règles*, p. 19) is: "The social fact is any manner of action, fixated or not, susceptible of exercising on the individual an exterior constraint"; or again: "The social fact is any manner of action which is general in the extent of a given society, while having its own existence independent of its individual manifestations."

His rule of observation is to consider social facts as things (*Règles*, p. 20). His rule of interpretation is "that the determining cause of a social fact ought always be sought among antecedent social facts, and not among states of the individual consciousness." (*Règles*, p. 135.) "Every time," he tells us (*Règles*, p. 128), "that a social phenomenon is directly explained by a psychic phenomenon we may rest assured that the explanation is false."

His theory of the social mind is worked out in the magazine article listed above. He believes that in the same way that the elements of psychic life combine to form a psychic whole, so the elements of social life combine to form a social whole. The life of representation is not able to exist save in the whole formed by the combination of its elements, and so the collective life does not exist save in the whole formed by the combination of the individuals (p. 296). These social states, however, "do not cease to be psychic, and it is indeed in them that one observes to best advantage the characteristic attributes of mentality" (p. 300). "It is a question simply of introducing and acclimating in sociology a conception parallel to that which tends more and more to prevail in psychology" (p. 301). "If one calls the distinctive quality of the representative life of the individual 'spiritual,' then one ought to say of the social life that it defines itself by a 'hyper-spirituality,' which means that we still find the distinctive attributes of psychic life, but raised to a higher power, in such manner as to constitute something entirely new" (p. 302). He would prefer instead of using the term collective psychology, to say straightway sociology. "La

psychologie collective, c'est la sociologie tout en-
tiére."

His definition of religion will be seen characteristic
of his general position, containing the elements of
exteriority and constraint (*Religion*, p. 47). "A
religion is a unified system of beliefs and practices
relative to sacred things, that is to say things set
apart and forbidden—beliefs and practices which
unite into one single moral community called the
church all those who adhere to them." It however
goes beyond the bare statement of what a social
fact is, in its fixing it firmly in a group. Durkheim
himself recognizes this progress of his point of view
in a footnote to the definition quoted in which he
says: "The obligation evidently comes from the
fact that these beliefs are the possession of a group
which imposes them upon its members." Throughout his discussion he insists that there is nothing
illusory about religion, that it is a social product,
that it represents the values of social life, that it is
at the school of collective life that the individual
has learned to idealize (p. 417, etc.).

From this he proceeds to develop his theory that
all conceptual thinking is social. "There are
scarcely any words among those we usually employ
whose meaning does not pass to a greater or less
extent the limits of our personal experience." If

concepts, collective representations, "belong to a whole social group, it is not because they represent the average of the corresponding individual representations: for in that case they would be poorer than the latter in intellectual content, while as a matter of fact they contain much that surpasses the knowledge of the average individual" (p. 434-5). "Society is not the illogical or a-logical incoherent and fantastic being it has often been considered to be, but on the contrary the collective form of consciousness is the highest form of the psychic life since it is the consciousness of consciousnesses" (p. 444). Of the fundamental categories which are social things, he says (p. 440): "They not only come from society itself, but the things which they express are of a social nature. Not only is it society which has founded them, but their contents are the different aspects of the social being: the category of class was at first indistinct from the concept of the human group. It is the rhythm of social life which is at the basis of the category of time. The territory occupied by the society furnished the material for the category of space. It is the collective force which was the prototype of the concept of efficient force, an essential element in the category of causality."

These quotations are not given either for approval

or condemnation but to show how widely and suggestively he uses his attitude towards social facts as realities of observation, even though he has to embody them in a social mind. Unlike many a writer we meet who believes in the social mind, and who thinks that with such belief he has done about all that is required of him, Durkheim merely posits this social mind as a resting place for his facts, and works all the harder. The resting place is not necessary any longer, but the work stands just as sound, or at least just as suggestive on the tests of his achievement in each particular field.

His use of volume and density in interpreting the division of social labor will be found in Book II, Chapter II of his work on that subject.

§ 61. Georg Simmel, 1858–1917, professor at the University of Berlin.

| | |
|---|---|
| Ueber soziale Differenzierung | 1890 |
| Die Probleme der Geschichtsphilosophie | 1893 |
| Einleitung in die Moralwissenschaft | 1893 |
| Philosophie des Geldes | 1900 |
| Soziologie | 1908 |

Since the text was written a much needed volume in English has appeared by N. J. Spykman under the title *The Social Theory of George Simmel*, which unfortunately I have not been able to use. Other recent discussions are Maria Steinhoff, "Die

Form als soziologische Grundkategorie bei Simmel,"
*Koelner Viertelsjahrshefte für Soziologie*, IV, p. 215.
V. Jankelevitch, Georg Simmel, Philosophe de la
Vie, *Rev de Mét. et de Morale*, 1925, pp. 213–57 and
373–86. Ingjald Nissen, "Vergesellschaftung als
Einstellung, Eine Betrachtung zu Simmel's Sozio-
logie," *Annalen der Philosophie*, V, p. 77.

Simmel's initial question in approaching the study
of society is whether there is any place for a sociology in addition to the special social sciences. His
answer is that there is, providing a special point
of approach is found which gets new values and
meanings out of the material. (*Soziologie*, p. 1–5.)
He finds this approach in the search for forms as
distinct from the study of content. The content
consists of everything present in the individuals
who are the immediate concrete location of all historical reality, in the way of impulse, interest, purpose, inclination (*Trieb, Interesse, Zweck, Neigung,
psychische Zuständlichkeit und Bewegung*) of such
nature as to influence and affect others or receive
influences and effects from them (p. 6). Viewing
the content in this way he would not call it directly
social. It appears social to him only as viewed in
the form of its interactions, its Miteinander, Für-
einander and Gegeneinander phases. Any society
is characterized by its netting of forms. Only the

search for these forms is a science of sociology. Unless the same form appears in different contents and the same content in various forms, we would not have a science, but these conditions are actually evident in society (p. 8).

With most subtle and cautious discussion, unequalled in any other attempt at the study of society in any land, Simmel examines all the difficult boundary questions surrounding his study of form, such questions as whether an actual or approximate sameness of forms is found, in what sense reality can be attributed to the forms, and in general how society itself may be regarded as possible, and what categories of thought are required in studying it. In the light of Simmel's work all the current glib and superficial discussions which we meet so often as to society and the individual, society and personality, the concepts of society, and so forth belong in the dark ages of the study.

Now if the investigation of forms is justified, what will we find? Naturally, he says, sociology has first examined the big institutions like family, state and church (p. 18). But in and through them run countless finer forms, comparable with the microscopic in physiology: and it is these that knit the whole process into one, forms of rivalry, of communal eating, of letter writing, of personal adornment, of doing favors and getting returns, are chance examples among the thousands.

The next question is: Is all this not social psychology? And his answer is (p. 21–3): The material is psychic but the study is not psychology. Purpose and meaning (Sinn und Absicht), of the study do not run to psychology, but direct on the configuration of the content (sondern auf diesen Inhalt und seine Konfigurationen selbst). He defends the reality of the material he studies even though it does not knit itself together in a closed space world (selbstständige Raumeswelt) and make itself visible to the senses (anschaulich). This query he carries out further (pp. 557–63) showing that this reality is not that of an oversoul, that the need of a psychic carrier (psychische Träger) of the facts is falsely assumed, and that the only proper sense for social psychology, would be, not that of study of an oversoul, but that of study of a particular subdivision of ordinary psychology, namely that of the interinfluencing of men in social life.

For Simmel's comparison of his forms with those of Euclid's geometry repeated passages in Chapter I of the Sociology should be examined. See especially page 12, where the limits of the analogy are indicated. "Both geometry and sociology leave to other sciences the investigation of the contents which are represented in their forms, as also they leave to other sciences the totalities whose mere forms they picture. It hardly needs mention that this analogy goes no further than to making plain the nature of this main problem of sociology. Geometry has the advantage of simple forms into which the complex forms can be analyzed. But in sociology such an analysis into simple forms is not for us to hope in any near future."

As an illustration of the type of study that might fall within Simmel's social psychology as a subdivision of psychology, one may refer to Allport, *Journal of Experimental Psychology*, 1920, p. 159, who describes laboratory tests of the way behavior varies (1) on direct response to a stimulus which is "some form of social behavior in others," and (2) in response to a "non-social stimulus" when response is modified by the presence of others.

The quotation in the text as to Simmel's failure to secure following will be found in *Logos*, VIII, 121. "Ich weiss dass ich ohne geistigen Erben sterben werde, und es ist gut so."

## XXI. Typical Attempts at Classification of Groups

§ 64. To illustrate the great mass of factors that need to be taken into account in an effort to fix an exact meaning for such a term as community, see Stuart A. Queen, "What is Community?" *Journal of Social Forces*, 1, p. 375–82.

§ 65. Cooley, *Social Organization*, p. 23. The primary groups "are chiefly primary in forming the social nature and ideals of the individual." Ellwood, *The Psychology of Human Society*, p. vi, says "Cooley has made it plain that the work of the sociologist must start with face-to-face groups." Types, to Cooley, are "any fairly distinct and durable detail of structure," and he finds types of personality, of classes, of religion, of language, of almost anything, (p. 22). Classes include "any persistent social group other than the family, existing within a larger group," (p. 209). An institution is "a definite and established phase of the public mind" (p. 313). Mr. Cooley's work has high recognized value in its field, but the lack of coherent criteria for classification, and the lack of interest in any such criteria, is all too plain. Hayes, in his *Introduction to the Study of Sociology*, pp. 74–5, contrasts on similar lines personal and impersonal groups, but makes these terms very closely equivalent in meaning to small and large. The small group of people known to one another, he says, is personal, "quite in contrast with the impersonality and anonymity of the city, and the larger public of state and nation." Miller, in a book called *Races, Nations and Classes,* remarks the identity in this respect between Cooley and Hayes, and proffers a step "forward" by a classification into vertical and horizontal groups; the former comprising the family, races, nations and religions; the latter, classes, castes, and groups which "in general are concerned with the conditions of economic life " (p. 14).

Charles A. Ellwood, *Introduction to Social Psychology,* pp. 118–23. Additional overlapping criteria are suggested by him in his book *The Psychology of Human Society,* 1925, pp. 117–21.

Maciver, *Community, a Sociological Study,* pp. 22, 23, 39, 128, 131. *The Elements of Social Science,* pp. 7–11. He says a community "is a focus of social life," an association its "organization" (*Community,* p. 24). "Every association, every organization of men, came into being through a covenant of men to establish it, and exists in a covenant of men to maintain it" (p. 128). The entire unreality of his position is clear enough. He has, in fact, reduced his classification to a humorous state in an appendix to his third edition (pp. 421–4), in which he attempts to get rid of the inconsistencies in his use of the terms individual, community and association (and these terms are structural to everything he has written), by elaborate lists of "attributes" which belong to each one of the terms exclusively, to any pair of them, or to all of them jointly. We are, for example, informed that the attributes, male and female, may apply to individuals but not to community or association, and the errors of others in this respect are pointed out. The atmosphere is that of the thirteenth century.

McDougall, *The Group Mind*, pp. 87–95. Compare MacDougall's classification with the current series in studies of progress referred to in Sec. 80, from instinct through custom to rational procedure. McDougall says the purpose of his classification is to secure "an aid to the discovery of general principles of collective life and the understanding of social life in general" (p. 88). The type of understanding he gets is illustrated by such statements as that "in commercial companies the group spirit commonly remains at the lowest level, for the dominant motive is industrial and financial gain" (p. 90); that among associations for public ends many "are *purely* altruistic or philanthropic" (p. 90); and that "the Hindu caste is a *pure* traditional group" (p. 92). The italics are mine.

Wieman, *International Journal of Ethics*, vol. 31, p. 381.

Pepper, *International Journal of Ethics*, vol. 32, p. 420.

Perry, *Journal of Philosophy*, vol. 21, p. 91.

Much light is thrown, it seems to me, on this whole question of the classification of group activity by two efforts, both of real value, which were not available to me when the text of this book was written. One is that of Floyd H. Allport, whose criteria are psychological in the sound coherent sense of individual function. The other is that of the British writer, F. C. Bartlett, who uses the instinct-interest-intelligence series, nominally drawn from individual psychology, though actually shot through with social content, but who uses it with thorough equipment and judgment, and without any of those lapses into verbal chaos common to discussions on this line.

Bartlett's proposals are to be found in the *International Journal of Ethics*, July, 1925, and are the outgrowth of his book, *Psychology and Primitive Culture*. The problem he sets himself is that of "the ways in which social behavior is determined directly by the modes of organization of the group." A group he defines as "any collection of people organized by some common appetite, instinctive or emotional tendency, need, interest, sentiment or ideal." This enumeration he holds to be complete, and to furnish the "typical organizing tendencies" which distinguish groups. In a legitimate series of

an evolutionary nature, beginning with the entire,
or almost entire, dominance of his lowest type of
group, he conducts us through the successive emergence of the higher types to the increasing importance
of the highest. This series is: I. The Instinct
Group, "organized by appetite or instinct, by some
dominant and violent emotional tendency or by
some powerful need" with "no evidence whatever
that in any but the most rudimentary sense, if
even in that, is the fitting of the behavior to the
situation consciously determined." II. The Interest and Sentiment Group, which "is essentially
a differentiated form from a larger social grouping
and which persists within this larger unit for a
period longer than the satisfaction of its *immediate*
organizing agency would seem to require." It de-
velopes into institutions, and while at the start its
"drive" pushes it along, at the end its institutional
aspect controls through fixed hierarchies of rank.
III.   The Ideal Group, for the reconciliation of the
interest groups.   This is "an organization of ways
of regarding a situation, of feeling in respect to that
situation, and of reacting towards it in such a manner
as to make the situation practically desirable."
The situation here is not merely a center for interest,
but "its significance comes uppermost."   Ideals he
regards as depending on formulations, while feel-

ings do not. Ideal groups refer not to the maintenance of the institutions of a particular group,
but either "(a) to a reconciliation of the different
institutions of a special group, and an attempt to
formulate their desirable future development; or
(b) to reconciling and similarly interpreting the institutions of more than one group." In ideal groups
he finds that social behavior takes a further step
towards freedom, and that social ranking tends to
abandon the institutional and show again the personality form. In the whole he shows us in an overlapping, evolutionary way, the instinct, interest and
ideal groups; their respective affective, institutional
and reactive capacities; their passage from fluidity
through stiffness to a new fluidity; and the advance
of social behavior towards freer forms. We have
here an interesting, and in some details a novel,
sketch of social development. What concerns us,
however, is only his method of classification, and
while many details within it could easily be challenged, I will content myself with asking Mr. Bartlett or any disputant on these lines the two following
general questions: first, are the terms taken from
individual psychology, or nominally so taken, really
the vital characterizing terms of the development?
And, second, looking at any primitive community,
not from the viewpoint of the problems, technique

and institutions of today, but from the viewpoint of its own environment, and its own size and activity, is it really so lacking in the "interest" and "ideal" group procedure as he alleges? Does it not within its own sphere have just as much of these as we have today?

While Bartlett's line of analysis is, it seems to me, inevitably doomed by the progress of social studies today, Allport, on the other hand, is a candidate for full control of the field, providing only that he can proceed to occupy it. When he has satisfied the psychologists as to his right to cut down through the instincts to his "prepotent reflexes," and stop there; and when he has satisfied himself as to just what he is doing when he adds consciousness to his social behavior, he has a clear clean position from which to advance to conquest. What is more he is exclusive in his tenure of this position so far as work in the United States is concerned: logically his book, *Social Psychology*, seems to stand strong and alone.

Allport starts solidly with the phenomenal, individual man as the sole and only subject of study. (See Afterword to the present book.) He violently denies that there exists any such thing as a group, in any of the senses in which sociologists commonly use the term, and he even goes so far as to produce a final standard of value out of his bio-psychical man, asserting that "the biological needs of the individual are the ends towards which his social behavior is a developed means" (p. 4). Social psychology is for him a part of the psychology of this individual, and through that psychology and that alone he proposes to interpret all of society. A group is defined by him as two or more persons who are assembled to perform some task, deliberate some proposal, or share some experience (p. 260). Through tests of psychology, as he has delimited it, he discriminates first between groups and crowds, and then, within the groups, between face-to-face and co-acting groups (p. 260). The crowd has a common object, but acts with emotional intensity under a primitive drive. With the face-to-face group, the individuals react mainly or entirely to one another, and the stimuli are therefore direct. With the co-acting group, the individuals are primarily occupied with some stimulus other than one another, and the social stimuli are merely "contributory." Here we seem to have, so far as they go, good sound psychological tests, not social content tests in psychological terms, or mixed criteria. But I need only to refer to Professor Woodworth's criticism in the *Journal of Abnormal Psychology*, April, 1925, made from a direct psychological point of view, that Allport's classification makes no place whatever for a fourth group type, "the most significant of social phenomena," namely team-work, where the log that two men are carrying or the ball and bat with which nine men are playing, is itself a part of the situation to be studied and classified. It is good to have the problem clear. Allport and his fellow workers deserve the best wishes of every sociologist, no matter how far they may succeed in going. His position towards his problem is very much more clear cut than that of the German worker in the same field, Hans Stoltenberg (*Sozio-psychologie*, 1914, *Seelgrupplehre*, 1922), so far as I am able to penetrate the terminology of the latter.

For other recent trials at classification, see Huard, *Les Classes Sociales, Revue International de Sociologie*, 28, 561, and Naville, De la solidarité des intérêts; *Revue Philosophique*, vol. 95, p. 167.

§ 66. Tönnies, *Gemeinschaft und Gesellschaft*, 1887, second edition, 1912; third edition, 1920. It was Tonnies' fate to be almost entirely neglected by students of society for over twenty years. Since the war, and since Simmel's death, he has come to be regarded as the outstanding leader of the German sociological movement, though the contrast between the workers who follow his type of approach, and those who follow more nearly Simmel's is ever more pronounced. His most important recent works in addition to many magazine articles, include *Kritik der öffentlichen Meinung*, 1922, and *Soziologische Studien und Kritiken*, 1925. See also his articles, *Annales de l'Institut International de Sociologie*, vol. VI and vol. X.

§ 68. Compare the structural arrangement of Ross's sociological works for classifications valuable for pedagogical purposes, but reduplicative and incoherent for any technical management of the material.

So far as concerns these various frames of reference for ordinary life, for professional uses, for the stimulation of audiences, and for many other purposes up to the most flexible of all for scientific statement, it is not impossible that some day we may be able to provide ourselves with something akin to the transformation formulas of physics, by which we may be able to transfer the meanings of one set into terms of another. We would get, not definite formulas, but channels or grooves of translation, for use in dealing with them. My early attempts in this field, made prior to the new world point of view in physics, and carried on, not without much struggle and strain, were of course unsatisfactory and were abandoned completely. They were not indeed attempts at transformation, but at fixation, and I am very glad indeed that I felt it in time to escape from them. Better barrenness, inaction, suspense, than imprisonment. Such transformation devices, if we get them, must grow out of the combined efforts of many workers over a protracted period; for their whole value will lie in the facilitation of common work and the securing of results interchangeable among the workers.

## XXII. Dominance: Clots: Survivals

§ 70. The word "realist" is of course often used with an implication different from that in the text. This involves the identification of the "realist" statesman with "the powers that be," and carries with it from the point of view of the opposing elements of society accusations of brutality and cynicism. The opposing elements find more need of a technique involving enthusiasms for ideals, justice, liberty and other similar representative expressions, and can less easily pass to an interpretative realistic expression of their activity in the sense in which the word is used in the text.

§ 71. See sections 26 and 23 preceding.

## XXIII. Friction: Revolution

§ 76. An interesting illustration of the extent to which interpretations in such terms can go, centering around the word "communist" is to be found in the address by the editor of one of our most important business newspapers before the convention of a national trade association in the spring of 1924 at the time of the investigations by Congress into acts of the departments of the interior and of justice. He enlarged upon the extent of communist organizations in the United States, said that the liberals in Congress were elected by radicals in their states, that the radicals were merely puppets of the communists, that the investigation of Teapot Dome was simply a "means of advancing distrust of government among the people," that "sound-thinking people should refuse to attach any merit to the charges against public officials," and concluded: "By education we can combat this movement. It is up to you business men to get it before it gets you. You spend hundreds of dollars in promoting sales and advertising. Why not spend money and time in building up the very foundation of business, which these radicals are trying to destroy?"

All this can readily be taken apart, analyzed and reduced to definite facts, which, as always, will not be what they seem. It is not here a question as to the sense in which he is right or wrong: it is a question of taking his assertions, connections, values, just as he gives them, and locating their meaning in social activity.

## XXIV.  Progress

§ 79.  A refreshing statement concerning progress in a particular field as made by a leading worker in that field can be found in the following passages from J. Vendryes, *Language*, p. 358; and they are not weakened for the present purpose by the fact that here as often in his more general statements he phrases his views in terms of "mentality" or similar words foreign to our own line of analysis. Assuming some human whirlpool through which languages should be mixed up until French or English passed "from the expression of the abstract to that of the concrete," and became "full of mystical and subjective categories," he asks:  "Would this be progress or decadence?", and he answers:  "Neither, at least if we treat the matter from the linguistic point of view."  He goes on to say:  "We need not consider the purely relative advantages or inconveniences of a change of civilization or even of a return to the state known as barbarism.  We have no right to consider a rational and abstract language because it happens to be our own as in any way superior to a mystical and concrete one.  It is entirely a question of two different types of mentality each of which may have its merits.  There is nothing to prove that in the eyes of an inhabitant of Sirius the civilized person's mentality does not represent degeneration."

§ 80. Concerning earthquakes, see Bretz, *Scientific Monthly*, March, 1924, p. 239.

For man as standard of value, see sec. 52, preceding.

For the development series from instinct and custom to rationality, see sections, 65 and 67.

### XXV. World Peace: Socio-Analysis

§ 83. We may take any book of the popular type, emphasizing our racial superiority, predicting the terrors of its overthrow, and urging its maintenance by whatsoever force and arms. Analysis of what is behind and beneath will come down to definite social activities, and the value the particular writer implicitly places on them. Bring this fully and exactly to light, weigh it in terms of other social activities, and such books will have little pretense left to their arrogance. It will then be for them what they really mean, not what universalizing pretenses they have, what concealed purposes they appeal to.

# AFTERWORD

# AFTERWORD

A survey of the publications bearing on the issues which have been under consideration in this book, since the text was written two years ago, shows much important development. On the one side, the new world aspect, deriving from physics, tends to become clearer and interpretatively more significant wherever it is used. On the other side, marked progress has been made, both in clearing away certain confusions in thought and phrase hurtful to social interpretation, and also, more especially in Germany, in systematizing knowledge of society from a coherent point of view; that is to say, scientifically, in the sense in which I have been using the word.

# I

## The Changing View of the World

More vividly even than before may we now see ourselves in the swelling currents of a new intellectual life. We see ourselves involved in the re-creation of a universe.  All things known to man, including himself, have been gaining new meanings, new fluidity, new functional values.  And this is not at all because some one phase, even some very great phase, such as was at its announcement the scientific theory of evolution, sheds far-reaching light, but because the entire process of the knowing and the known is now functioning—I believe I may truthfully say for the first time in human history—within a system of what we have come to call science: a system of expression of which every part, every term and every meaning is willing to submit itself fully and freely to the tests of the other parts, the other terms and the other meanings, for its application, its validity, its survival.

Brilliantly this is shown to us in Whitehead's *Science and the Modern World*, and in such works as Max Planck's, *A Survey of Physics*, and Russell's *A, B, C of Relativity*.  Whitehead's very theme is this new fertility of knowledge in contrast with the mechanical material frame of scientific work of the Galilean-Newtonian age now drawing to a close, and he traces the emergence of the new world view richly and intimately in its wide meanings, and so in marked contrast with the narrower conventional lines followed in Part I of the present book.  All of these new works show us the world of relativity, the

world of quanta, and the world in which the principle
of least action has been advancing from its status
of technician's formula to a wide vividness of understanding.

This new world view which in crude phrase may
be said to have been born with Einstein's general
relativity is already far past dependence on the
fate of Einstein's own specific work. If Dayton C.
Miller's long and faithful observations at high alti-
tudes announced to us in terms of a measured ether
drift—and therefore challenging outright the re-
liability of the critical Michelson experiment, and
with it challenging the entire structure of "optical
relativity," as Birkhoff calls the Einstein physics—
should stand as they are, they may effect the Einstein computations, but they will not overthrow the
new world background that has become clear since
Einstein. Miller's results (see *Science*, vol. 61, p. 617,
and his 1925 address to the American Association
for the Advancement of Science, of which an abstract is published in *Science*, Jan. 29, 1926) are
accepted flatly in terms of an ether drift by Silberstein and described by him as "entirely antagonistic
to the Einstein relativity theory" (*Nature* 115, p.
798): while Eddington (*Nature* 115, p. 870), retorts
even more positively that whatever it is Miller has
observed, it cannot be an ether drift, for then all

the daily measurements at every astronomical observatory in the world would be distorted and valueless. Accepted interpretation is lacking within the special range, but in the broader range there is far too much construction already carried on to anticipate an overthrow from such a source as this. The Miller results if maintained must expect interpretation somehow within the new world view.

"The principle of relativity," Planck writes (pp. 67–8), "simply discards a form which owing to the advance of science was already out of date. In place of the old confined structure it erects a new one, more comprehensive and lasting." And Whitehead says (p. 173) on the basis of his wide survey: "It is therefore necessary to reformulate the law (of gravitation) in a way which does not presuppose any particular space-time system, and Einstein has done this." Russell adds his testimony (p. 142), speaking of the empirical confirmations of Einstein: "But if Einstein's law had not been found to agree with experience we could not have gone back to Newton's law. We should have been compelled by logic to seek some law expressed in terms of tensors, and therefore independent of our choice of coordinates."

That Einstein had various alternative procedures open to him when he attacked his problem is well

enough known; and so in contrast to the many
physicists who welcomed his advance and strove to
transform their work into the new terms with all
possible speed, we find very naturally a small number of men who emphasize the uncertainty of Einstein's choice of alternatives, question his three or
four delicate confirmations, and not only hold to
the old forms, but proclaim them to be the true ones
because their own personal work still seems readily
to fit into them.   In this whole matter of the present
acceptance of Einstein and of the new outlook, one
can easily see the influence on this man and on that
of what is so commonly called temperament, but
what is really the complex personal meeting point
of very numerous lines of activity.   Interestingly
enough this appears in the phrase of the geologist,
Chamberlin, in his introduction to Charles Lane
Poor's *Gravitation versus Relativity* (p. xviii), as he
speaks of "that gloomy forecast of Minkowski"
that space and time separately will prove to be
but shadows, and that only the union of the two
will show independent.   Gloomy indeed to a geologist whose life time work is spread before him in
tactile forms; and gloomy to a physicist like Lodge
who, for the sake of keeping spirits, must also
keep matter.   But on the other hand cheering and
stimulating to workers with a world of electricity

or heat or atomic constitution before them; and to all workers among the phenomena of man in society who so long have sought a clarified way of stating and examining the brutish and confused deliveries of their senses.

To sum up the meaning of all this for the social sciences, I may quote first, Planck, that hard working physicist of the laboratory and the computation pad, who (p. 115) writes, not dogmatically, but as an expression of present status: "Thus by referring to a finite time interval the motion at any instant is investigated with the help of a later motion, and present events are in a certain manner made dependent upon later events, and the principle (that of least action) acquires a teleological character": and again (p. 126), "Anyone desiring to regard the principle of least action as mechanical would today have to apologize for doing so." And then Russell; (p. 214) who after describing the way an electron is known by its "effects" goes on to say: "But the word effects belongs to a view of causation which will not fit modern physics, and in particular will not fit relativity"; and again: "It is not true that the past determines the future in some sense other than that in which the future determines the past: the apparent difference is only due to our ignorance because we know less about the future than about the past." And, finally, Whitehead (p. 103) who, after speaking of events as they mirror contemporary events and as they mirror the past, proceeds: "An event has a future. This means that an event mirrors within itself such aspects as the future throws back onto the present, or, in other words, as the present has determined concerning the future. Thus an event has anticipation." Such quotations, I repeat, are not so much philosophizing about physics as reporting conditions in actual physical investigation today, their foundation resting in the actual laboratory use of the principle of least action.

Alfred North Whitehead: *Science and the Modern World*, 1925.
Max Planck: *A Survey of Physics*, 1925.
Bertrand Russell: *The A, B, C of Relativity*, 1925.

## II

### Instincts as Interpretative Agents

The clearing up of a typical confusion of a nature seriously harmful to social interpretation has come in connection with a dispute over instincts which has been active in American philosophical, psychological and sociological publications for about five years. The main credit for this clearing must go to McDougall who developed a system of instincts for the explanation of society of such meretricious charm as to fascinate every investigator seeking the easiest way with social facts, and to Bernard who with years of labor tore the system to pieces, and revealed convincingly the naïveté with which it read into itself in advance all that it tried to explain.

McDougall is a psychologist who seems never to have sensed in the slightest degree the characteristics of a problem in social interpretation. The world to him is the situs of human beings who, as individuals, are not merely bio-psychic in Euclidean space, but are psychically tangible; their psyches have a solidity and firmness, a sort of muscular structure that one can get at and operate with. (Compare Planck on the anthropomorphic muscular analogy in the Force of the old physics, *op. cit.* pp. 6, 9, 27, 68). I have no quarrel with this view except in the one matter of its practical operation in the present stage of the investigation of society; but that practical operation is exactly what McDougall undertook. He described and classified a set of instincts in his individual man through which society was to be explained, regarding them more as motor mechanisms at first, then with a fuller telic (hormic) character. Without such instincts, he held, we would be deprived of all possibility of building up an intelligible account of character and volition; much less could anything social be explained without them: and this despite the fact that he had finally yielded to his critics far enough to admit that "the existence of instincts in man must always remain an hypothesis."

McDougall's book was extremely popular and went through a dozen or more editions.  But McDougall himself was compelled to vary his classification of instincts from time to time; and it also appeared that no two men could agree on any classification of instincts from this point of view; very quickly each and every one of the alleged instincts was sharply challenged by some investigator as meaningless and absurd.  Worse than that, discussion and interpretation of society carried on in terms of these instincts developed nothing more valuable than the output of any philosophizing busy-body.  The situation had to be looked into.

Psychologists took hold, both in their technical study of function, which does not concern us at the moment, and in their analyses with social content included.  Kuo sharply denied the existence of instincts, and proposed to substitute elementary units of reaction.  Dewey, from an initial approval advanced to a destructive transformation by emphasizing habits built up upon original endowments, not believing that an analysis of original endowments could be helpful socially, but still keeping them at the basis of his structure. Woodworth suggested a more functional statement in terms of drives. Dunlap came to regard the instincts as arbitrary classifications made to fit the logical purposes, or sometimes even the whims, of the classifier; and he substituted "desires" which he characterized as "actual organic conditions," but which his critics quickly identified as merely instincts under another name. Tolman, thoroughly examining and classifying all instinct theories from the psychologist's point of view, and himself upholding one such theory, could in the end hardly make a stronger statement than that "the facts demand some sort of instinct hypothesis," and that "the teleological hypothesis with its allowal of more or less innate patterns as required would seem to satisfy this demand as well as any." Josey from a logical, rather than a psychological, approach showed why instincts should not be regarded as "forces," and why cultures were poorly explained in terms of capacities. Ayres, with a humorous analysis fully deserved by the instinct theorists, not only provided them with the definition that for them "an instinct in man is his disposition to behave whatever way he may

behave ": but constructively went so far as to assert
that "the social scientist has no need of instincts:
he has institutions": and again: "human behavior
is the behavior of institutions."

The full overthrow came from sociologists like
Bernard who insisted on knowing what kind of help
was given their own problems by instincts, or from
psychologists like Allport who directly faced the
social function in the individual, and like Kantor
who introduced a very large amount of social material into their work, not confusedly but with a hard-
boiled intention to see clearly what it was they
were doing. There emerged with a new vividness
the issues of original endowment versus acquired
habit, of individual versus institutional statement,
of individual centering of attention versus social
centering.

Bernard's exhaustive studies of what was actually
being done with instincts of the McDougall type
in social investigation fill a large volume. The result was an overwhelming exhibit of the way in
which social facts were being treated as individual
habits and read back into individual instincts which
were then treated as "forces" of an illegitimate
type and made to explain the material out of which
they had been evoked. He did not reject instinct
entirely as an aid to interpretation, but held that

only by reducing it to its lowest terms, after demolishing the "verbal concepts" of McDougall, could the sociologist make an "investigation of the underlying and much more simple and elementary constituent natural processes of man," and use the resulting forms as "building stones of character."

Allport's concern is with man acting socially, and yet he proposes to treat that man from a strict psychological point of view. His man is a bio-psychical man in Euclidean space, and his psychology is throughout individual psychology, with social psychology, as a strictly included functional branch. His logical consistency in this respect, unparalleled, so far as I know, in America, is what gives him his high value here. He rejects flatly all groups and group concepts as used by sociologists and proposes to define and classify whatever variations there are in the ways two or more men act when together in terms of their individual psychology. (See Comment to Chapter XXI of this book.) He rejects the McDougall type of instinct, carries out the Bernard demand for simple elements by a theory of pre-potent reflexes (elaborated, however, into capacities, driving forces, and habit trends built up out of them) regards everything social as merely similarities of individuals, and proceeds to do very valuable work in his field.

Kantor's objective was to build a psychology out of the "actual observable events" consisting of responses and stimuli, and doing this he finds one great class of stimuli to be social, "the reaction of persons to specifically group conditions." Instincts he rejected as animistic, and social causes he held could not be found within individuals. Studying types of reaction when the social stimuli were reached in his system he classified contingential, cultural and idiosyncratic, and to the cultural or institutional stimuli he gave a most important position. In the actual psychological process, he says, a great place is held by "the action of persons upon changes in national or other group phenomena." This centering of attention on the institutional and this definite working out of it as stimulus within a psychology, is a great gain, but it is to be noted that Kantor still shows a certain wavering of vision; as when he becomes compelled to make a double statement about social stimulus; since along with the quotation above that it is "the reaction of persons to specifically group conditions" he places an alternative phrase; "specific reactions common to numbers of individuals or collectivities": a wavering, unavoidable from his point of view, and common to many of the clearest visionings of social fact that we find in current literature. His very specification of what he means by responses and stimulus, "the responses," namely, "of psychological organisms and the stimulus objects or conditions which interact with them," contains a series of problem-words that indicate well enough how much further analysis is requisite.

To summarize the results of this fight over instincts, we may give compactly the positions of the four leading writers described, and add to them that of Ellwood, perhaps the most clearly organized of American pedagogical sociologists; the characterization to be understood, however, only from the point of view of the one problem which concerns this book.

McDougall: His men are not merely bio-psychical, nor Euclidean, but psychic in a certain forceful, muscular way. Once get down to the underlying individual characteristics of these psychic men, and you have explained the things we mean when we talk of society.

Allport: His men are sharply bio-psychical, and Euclidean. They have minds in that order and are set in nature. Center your attention on them, and they will take care of themselves. Finish your study of them and you will know all there is to know about society.

Ellwood: Starts with observational society and social man in it. Analyzes along both lines, but

without sharp separations. Fits the two lines together smoothly, for professional purposes. In the
end interprets the society by the man, for otherwise,
he thinks, we would have nothing but a biology or
physics of society.

Bernard: Starts with society observationally.
Examines its interpretations by use of the man in
it, and breaks these interpretations down. Demands something very simple indeed out of that
man before it is available for use in interpreting
society.

Kantor: Starts with man observationally. Examines his stimuli and responses. Finds society in
the form of institutions a most astoundingly important stimulus, and holds that its study can be
perfected as stimulus.

From my own point of view, it seems to me that
Bernard, Allport and Kantor all present to us, if
not approaches to the position taken in this book,
at least approximations to some better unified position under which social facts can be more surely and
delicately analyzed. Bernard is unquestionably
under obligation to carry his analysis still further,
and if he does this, it seems to me he cannot stop
till he reaches the simple statement that he deals
just with activity, with something going-on in and
across man-society. Allport is free to pursue his

admirable line of investigation, without hampering himself with the Euclidean dogmatism of an assertion that his type of deliveries are the only type of scientific deliveries that can be produced from the social field. Kantor can carry on a similar psychology, specializing in his own way in the social stimuli, and at the same time recognize that the whole cultural-institutional situation may have as definite a visibility and as definite a possibility of direct analysis as has the stimulus-response situation seen in the individual. Whether these men will tend to develop in this direction depends of course on whether they can see—or, perhaps better said, whether any one can in reality see—the social situations through the individuals direct and clear, without dominance under the various nominalist-realist, subjective-objective, actor-environment distinctions: and whether, when visualizing thus, scientific treatment will prove its right to exist by clarity and orderliness of results.

William McDougall:     *An Introduction to Social Psychology*, 1908: 14th ed., 1921 (pp. 45–89);
*Outline of Psychology*, 1923 (pp. 71–73);
"The Use and Abuse of Instinct in Social Psychology":
*Journal of Abnormal and So-*

*cial Psychology*, 16 (p. 286: p. 332).

"Can Sociology and Social Psychology Dispense with Instincts?" *Ib.* vol. 19 (p. 40).

Zing Yang Kuo: "Giving Up Instincts in Psychology." *Journal of Philosophy*, 18 (p. 645).

John Dewey: *Human Nature and Conduct*, 1922.

Robert S. Woodworth: *Dynamic Psychology*, 1918.

Knight Dunlap: *Elements of Scientific Psychology*, 1922 (pp. 209–23).

*Social Psychology*, 1925 (pp. 15–16).

E. C. Tolman: "The Nature of Instinct," *Psychological Bulletin*, 1923 (p. 215).

C. C. Josey: *The Rôle of Instinct in Social Philosophy*, 1921.

C. E. Ayres: "Instinct and Capacity." *Journal of Philosophy*, 1921 (pp. 563, 565, 603).

L. L. Bernard: *Instinct, A Study in Social Psychology*, 1924 (p. 533).

Floyd H. Allport· *Social Psychology*, 1924 (pp. vi, 42, 49, 140, 260, 396).

J. R. Kantor: *Principles of Psychology*, 1924 (pp. xv, xvi, 11, 44, 50, 123, 155–8, 167–70, 188, 214–5).

"How is a Science of Social Psychology Possible?" *Journal of Abnormal and Social Psychology*, 17 (p. 65, p. 77).

"What are the Data and Problems of Social Psychology?" *Journal of Philosophy*, 20 (p. 457).

Charles A. Ellwood: *The Psychology of Human Society*, 1925 (p. 15).

### III

### The Organization of Knowledge of Society

Leopold von Wiese is the sociologist who has made the most striking advance by systematizing for the first time our technical knowledge of society, not along nature-philosophizing lines, nor again along the shuttle-track dualizing lines, but in a coherent system from a unified point of view. So important do I regard his work, and so entirely in accord with the tendency for which I have been arguing—and this, whether he likes my attitude towards his psychological references or not—that, had my text not been in type before I gained acquaintance with him, I would have been tempted to recast considerable portions of it with close attention to his work.

Wiese's book is *Allgemeine Soziologie*, Part I, *Beziehungslehre*, 1924. His *Gebildelehre*, which is to form Part II of the completed work, has not yet been published. The exact issues in question can hardly be understood, however, without close examination in connection with his four preliminary discussions in the *Koelner Vierteljahrshefte für Soziologie,* 1921–3. I shall assert (1) that his entire treatment is in terms of unified purposeful activity; (2) that his developing statement about what he is actually doing amounts to a recognition of this; but (3) that he has not yet cast aside a number of confusing, so-called underlying, views and terms about men and things, through which he strives to interpret himself towards or relate himself to the philosophies, psychologies and sociologies in their various branches, and towards common speech forms.

Wiese starts with Simmel's forms of socialization. But he does not like their Euclidean abstractness. He transfers them into Beziehungen, relations, viewed as existing between men viewed as similarly existing; not mere logical relations, but "something doing," something going on, Handeln, activity. In what follows I shall use his own technical German terms, and Beziehung is to be taken in this sense throughout. Alongside the Beziehungen he set Gebilde, institutions, in three stages, Massen, crowds, Gruppen, groups, and "abstrakte Kollektivitäten," collectivities, such as church or state. The Gebilde are ideas in the minds of individual men, and yet they also participate in the going quality, the Handeln; he treats them as activity, but he still, even in his latest writings, wavers a little in characterizing them.

Now here is an outline of what has happened to him in the course of his work.

1. At first he analyzed the Beziehungen into those of the first order, between two or more men and those of the second order, between men and Gebilde; along with which he analyzed the theory of Gebilde into a theory of the Gebilde themselves and one of the Beziehungen between them. At his very first touch therefore Beziehungen showed signs of going all the way up, and Gebilde of coming all the way back.

2. Next he found that every social situation that he studied—or let us say almost everyone, for I am not sure just exactly how far even today he would carry this proposition through towards its limit in the abstract collectivities, though this is involved in calling society itself as well as each Beziehung a Vorgang—appeared as process from some point of view with reference to other situations. He introduced the term Prozesse between Beziehungen and Gebilde.

3. Almost at once the Prozesse identified themselves with the Beziehungen; there was no way to hold them apart. He therefore soon made the two

terms exact equivalents, and so defined them repeatedly, and continues to define them. But for
practical purposes of investigation he differentiates
working usages for the two terms. Let Beziehungen
be the Beziehungen of the first order, as one finds
them between two or more men regarded as individuals, without presupposing the presence of previously
formed Gebilde. Let Prozesse be the Beziehungen
of the second order, which go on within the Gebilde.

4. As he proceeded with his work of assembling,
analyzing and classifying social situations, something surprising happened. The Gebilde began to
appear in between the technical Beziehungen and
the technical Prozesse, without waiting for their
due time to appear later on in his system. He had
to recognize them there, although he does it grudg-
ingly, calling them by preference Zustände, which
we may translate as situations that are going to
be Gebilde some day.

Before going further with this examination of his
development, let us look at his work more concretely. He presents us a large table of six or
seven hundred typical Beziehungen and Prozesse
and the description of the contents of this table
makes up the bulk of his book. His great line of
analysis divides all social situations or activities
(these two descriptive words are not his, but mine;

he himself uses either Beziehungen or Prozesse in what he calls "the wider sense") into joining activities and splitting activities; under the Beziehungen proper he gives us (a) those that are Zu-und Miteinander (towards and with one another), and (b) Aus- und Ohn- (originally Gegen-) einander, (away from and against, or without one another); but also he needed a third group, (c) the mixed, which appeared compositely "with and against." Under the Prozesse a similar division is given, into the differentiating and integrating, to which are added two more complex types, the destroying, leading to ruin, and the up-building leading to reconstruction. For illustration, starting with contacts, such as touching, glancing, blushing, jesting, or in secondary form such as telephoning or writing; he gives us Beziehungen such as devoting, crediting, hurrahing, agreeing; then integrating processes like naturalizing, legitimatizing and taming; and finally reconstructing processes like symbolization, dogmatization, policing, traditionalizing and office-creating; while in between the Beziehungen and Prozesse he inserted attitudes (like sociality and dependence) and the Zustände or budding Gebilde in crowd, group and collectivity forms.

For the material which he uses Wiese gives credit to the rich and varied, though unsystematized, ob-

servations and descriptions of Ross, and to the
accumulations by Waxweiler of vocabularies of
words with sociological values. Both of these men
he joins with Simmel as the pioneers who made his
work possible, but if it is his systematization that is
important to us, then it is solely from Simmel that
he derives, for he rejects entirely the nature-philo-
sophical trend of Waxweiler; while the psychological
aspects that he takes over from Ross occupy, I think,
a completely quiescent place in his investigations,
and are among the phases which, I will proceed
to show, are in line to be dropped out entirely.

5. Along with this development of his analysis
of social situations, Wiese gave a great deal of
attention to putting himself right with psychology.
He was handicapped in this, first by the prominence
of the substantial "Seele" in all German psychology
and philosophy, and secondly by the dominance of
psychological sociology among the American writers
from whose extended studies he drew so much
material, and with whose attitude he seems to feel
himself unable to break, however much he has subordinated it. His approach on this side lay in
examining his word Beziehung for its psychological
and logical values, and he at once rejected any
interpretation of the term in a merely logical sense,
and as well any interpretation of it as a mere

annex to individual psychology. He presented a scheme as follows: Psychology appears first as a general study of mind; then as individual psychology, a study of mental processes in men as considered apart from other men; next as socio-psychology, in which men are taken with respect to fellow men; then as psycho-sociology, where men are taken under a "synoptische" observation; and then, right along in the same series, he places the Beziehungslehre, and the theories of the Prozesse and the Gebilde. It is here of the greatest significance that on repeated occasions he has listed the methods to be used in social studies under five operations, as follows: describing, analyzing, measuring, comparing and systematizing; every one of these is a clean cut operation within the material itself, and may be understood in no other way, especially when in connection we consider his repeated rejection of interpretations through underlying "forces," specified by him to include "seelische" interchanges.

So far all is well, barring the necessity of so many stages in the series (and probably barring the psycho-sociology altogether), if the psychology is to be taken in the sense of American behaviorism, rather than soul-substance study. It is all on the surface, all clean cut, no hidden tricks. And, as J have said, his own work is entirely in line with such a reading of it. But here is where his trouble enters. He is still bothered by the distinction between subjective and objective, not for a moment in doing his own work, but very much indeed in his endeavors to set himself right with writers using a dualistic terminology. He introduces the subjective-objective distinction in connection with the stage of methodological analysis, he struggles industriously with Handeln seen subjectively and Handeln seen objectively, with the Beziehungen and the Gebilde from the two points of view. He accepts as essential McDougall's instincts, although he does not practise their use at all. He develops an attitude towards psychology, subjectively considered, as showing only the "seelische Wurzel" (root) of what happens in society, but as not directly lying in point in its study. He says at times that there are moving forces;—on the one side, external Einflüsse, on the other, innere Antriebe,—despite his previous denials that sociology can depend on them. And with it all it is perfectly clear in his mind that Handeln, the active situation, the very material of his study, is not merely a phenomenon of "Sein" but also one of "Funktion"; that is, that it is purposive, that it looks forward as well as back, just as it comes to him to be studied. His psychological factors, in truth, seem merely to occupy the rather amusing place in his investigations, which Dunlap allots to the "ego" in his own work, when he writes of it (*Elements of Scientific Psychology*, p. 26): "It is not far from the truth to say that in psychology we acknowledge the ego in order to ignore it in our further scientific work."

If I have given a true analysis of Wiese's work, I do not need to say anything more. It is apparent that the husks of the old forms of speech are ripe to drop off of his theory, thereby freeing it, not only from annoyance within, but also from destruction under the hands of other workers who try to force those aspects back upon him. And yet I may be able to make the point still clearer by a few words concerning another comparable recent German work on general sociology, Alfred Vierkandt's, *Die Gesellschaftslehre*. Vierkandt, like Wiese, connects himself closely to Simmel, but unlike Wiese, he proceeds to destroy Simmel instead of enriching him. While Wiese's special studies have been in the field of modern social problems, Vierkandt's have been in anthropology; and he is infested with the "Seelenleben der Naturvölker," which merely means with something personified at too great a sociological distance from the observer. Simmel's forms become to Vierkandt merely

a name for a closely delimited study. Vierkandt
goes direct to Tönnies, the outstanding leader in
interpretations in terms of generalized will and
intellect, emphasizing Tönnies' contrast of Gemeinschaft and Gesellschaft as objective fact. He takes
from Durkheim the worst feature of the latter's
position, the flesh and blood social objectivity; he
uses Tarde on his substantially psychological side,
and he gulps McDougall whole (pp. 1–5). The
great problems are to him the specific forces behind
society, and the nature of the inner unification (die
Art der inneren Verbundenheit), (p. 14). The theory
of Social Wholes is his heart's treasure: "Gebilde in
which the whole determines causally all the details":
"Every whole is something fully individual" (p. iv).
"Interactions (Wechselwirkungen) must have inner
foundation, or, as we may say instead, they must
be of soul-type" (p. 34). Thereby he gains for
himself and his followers the sense of reality in
society he seeks. Thereby for me he deals only with
phantasms. And it is noteworthy that while one
careful German student, Max Rumpf, presents long
lists of similarities between Wiese and Vierkandt,
and thinks they can be harmonized, Wiese himself,
contrary to his usual catholicity of appreciation,
attacks Vierkandt vigorously for his insistence on
building sociology out of inner individual traits,

for his "Psychologismus," and denies that he has presented a real sociology at all. It is, I believe, either one thing or the other, with no middle ground; either Vierkandt with his body-like psyche, or Wiese, stripped of a few remaining bad verbal camp-followers, with a clean sociology of men in function together.

\*    \*    \*    \*    \*    \*    \*

A recent American book, notable for its emphasis on group activity as the central field of theoretical sociology, and for its desire to work out practical methods for its investigation, is Lindeman's *Social Discovery*. Lindeman defines a group as two or more men "consciously acting together for the purpose of advancing a mutual interest" (p. 207). This is of course superficial and vague, for the phrase, "consciously acting together" will not stand the slightest analysis, but it roughly indicates one type of group—such as, for example, a cooperative marketing association during its period of formation—and we can accept his work in this special field. He goes far enough to include what a group is doing (that is, its activity as observed on the surface), and what it thinks it is doing (p. 190) in his study, but cuts it off there.

What is significant is that he finds he cannot get anywhere in this study except by taking the whole

# Afterword

subject matter under the rubric of activity. He
rejects instincts for interpretative purposes (p. 165),
and the possibility of building up social habits out
of individual habits (p. 166), and finds himself in
"reaction to subjective interpretations of group behavior" (p. 117). He studies leadership as a function of the group, modes of representation, modes
of consent, the use of experts in a group, and the
use of participating and non-participating observers
for the purpose of getting information about the
group. He sees the "conjunction of activity and
purpose" (p. 197), the importance of "point of
view," understood in the sense of long or short
point of view (p. 231), the nature of the interests
in the group and the representation of these interests (p. 139), the conflicts of interests, and rights
as the evaluation of interests (p. 142), the measurements of power, and the cross sectional qualities
of public opinion (p. 348) and of group analysis
(p. 358), and the interpretation of activities in the
terms of one another. Barring the definition and
limitation of field, I am reasonably familiar with
all this type of work, including the terminology;
and I should be the last one to fail in approval.

But there is another side to Lindeman's book
which is very different. He surrounds all of his
work with the phrasings of a naïve and popularizing

psychology, which lead him to describe power as the non-intellectual and non-ethical means used by the group (p. 233); to use the stimulus and response categories in such a way as to make the environment be the "cause" of the beginning of formation of the group (p. 147); to see customs, mores, traditions largely in this outlying field of environmental stimuli (Chap. XIII); and to see the group as only a means to the ends of the individuals (p. 112: 138). From the same source arises his limitation of the field of study, as given above.   Labor is not a group unless specifically organized (p. 134); five thousand individual farmers "mean nothing to the social scientist" unless they are organized (p. 122), but then they "mean everything" to him.   He thus fences himself in both as to the field of phenomena,— the group activities as they are defined on first inspection,—and as to the activities within that field which he is willing to recognize as running through them and being part of them.   And all by outworn psychological tests.   But it is the work he actually does, not the limitation on it, that is the important and valuable thing.

Just as I used Vierkandt to show better the values of Wiese, so now in contrast to Lindeman, I will briefly refer to another book of the same year, *The Basis of Social Theory* by A. G. A.

Balz. Balz is strong in the phases to which Lindeman has given no connected thought, but he never
arrives at recognizing the existence of the problems
of study that Lindeman is actually working on.
Balz gives us a fluent description of man and
society together; and he holds that the distinction
between the individual and the social is not basic
(p. 32); that the facts called individual are themselves social (p. 40); that individual psychology is
an abstraction (p. 44); that the basic data of psychology are social facts, and the basic form of
psychology is social psychology (p. 45).   He follows
this with a similar discussion of original nature and
nurture, finding these two terms both applicable
to every fact of human experience, and unreal when
sharply opposed to one another (Chapter II).

Thus far the beam of light he is emitting takes
its steady course.   But like Einstein's light as it
approaches matter in space, in other words as it
approaches the activities of society, it shows sharp
curvature.   The true social forces, he begins to
find, are to be found in human nature in the sense
in which he had defined it (p. 76); original nature
defines the limits of the possible (p. 99); in the final
analysis thought must pass from activities and functions to original nature (p. 109); the transformation
of human life as a biological fact to that life as

humanly social is the achievement in the final analysis of mind (p. 249). In short, swinging far to the one side for all technical purposes, Balz constructs human character under social conditions, and presents it to us as the basis of social theory, and thereby implicitly, though not explicitly, as the very substance of all social theory itself. How little he envisages a straightway, direct human situation, other than in terms of human character, may be read in the very paucity of his remarks on institutions (p. 75). I do not for a moment deny that a full statement of all phenomena may be made in Balz's terms; so also may the whole world be studied and analyzed and depicted in shades of a single color, red, or yellow, or blue. One of America's great artists has actually done this, has experienced the world in color after color; but that artist did not stop on any of these levels. Mr. Lindeman's exhibits alone are sufficient to show that Mr. Balz's line of thought is not the basis of social theory.

*  *  *  *  *  *  *

From this survey of recent developments, I think it may reasonably be concluded that psychology will tend to become a study of stimulus and reaction; while sociology will become a study of dimensions in a sense akin to that in which the physicist uses that term. By that contrast the two sciences may perhaps be given definitions under which they can maintain themselves sharply discriminated.

Leopold von Wiese: *Allgemeine Soziologie: I, Beziehungslehre*, 1924.
"Zur Methodologie der Beziehungslehre," *Koelner Vierteljahrshefte für Soziologie*, I, 1, p. 47.
"Das Psychische in the gesellschaftlichen Beziehungen," *Ib.*, I, 3, p. 66.
"Skizze des Aufbaues eines Systems der Beziehungslehre," *Ib.*, II, 4, p. 61.
"Die Tafel der menschlichen Beziehungen," *Ib.*, III, p. 250.
"A Vierkandts Gesellschaftslehre," *Ib.*, III, p. 176.
(NOTE: No page references to Wiese's work have been given in the text, though direct translation of his words has been largely used in describing him. Not textual reference, but only a thorough analysis of his development will bring out the essential points.)

Alfred Vierkandt: *Gesellschaftslehre*, 1923.
"Programm einer formalen Ge-

sellschaftslehre," *Koelner Veri-teljahrshefte*, I, 1, p. 55.

"Die Beziehung als Grundkate-gorie des soziologischen Den-kens," *Archiv für Rechts- und Wirtschafts-philosophie*, IX, p. 83.

Max Rumpf:        "Von rein formaler zu typolo-gisch-empirischer Soziologie," *Schmoller's Jahrbuch*, vol. 48, p. 917.

"Leopold von Wieses Bezie-hungslehre," *Ib.*, vol. 49, p. 193.

Eduard C. Lindeman:   *Social Discovery*, 1924.

A. G. A. Balz:        *The Basis of Social Theory*, 1924.

# INDEX
## RELATIVITY IN MAN AND SOCIETY

361